Carlos Maria Galli

CHRIST, MARY, THE CHURCH, AND THE PEOPLES

Pope Francis' Mariology

LIBERIA EDITRICE VATICANA

Published in Australia by

© Copyright 2019 Coventry Press

Coventry Press
33 Scoresby Road
Bayswater Vic. 3153
Australia

Original title: *El Evangelio de la Misericorida en espiritu de discernimiento. La etica social del papa Francisco*

Translated from Spanish by Luis Antonio Gallo
Translated into English by Salesians of Don Bosco of the Province of Mary Help of Christians of Australia and The Pacific

ISBN 9780648497707

© Copyright 2017 - Libreria Editrice Vaticana
00120 Città del Vaticano
Tel. 06.698.81032 - Fax 06.698.84716
commerciale.lev@spc.va

All rights reserved. Other than for the purposes and subject to the conditions prescribed under the *Copyright Act*, no part of this publication may be reproduced, stored in a retrieval system, or transmitted in any form or by any means, electronic, mechanical, photocopying, recording or otherwise, without the prior permission of the publisher.

Cataloguing-in-Publication entry is available from the National Library of Australia http:/catalogue.nla.gov.au/.

Printed in Australia

www.coventrypress.com.au

SERIES
THE THEOLOGY OF POPE FRANCIS

JURGEN WERBICK: *God's Weakness for Humankind.* Pope Francis' view of God

LUCIO CASULA: *Faces, Gestures and Places.* Pope Francis' Christology

PETER HÜNERMANN: *Human Beings According to Christ Today.* Pope Francis' Anthropology

ROBERTO REPOLE: *The Dream of a Gospel-inspired Church.* Pope Francis' Ecclesiology

CARLOS GALLI: *Christ, Mary, the Church and the Peoples.* Pope Francis' Mariology

SANTIAGO MADRIGAL TERRAZAS: *'Unity Prevails over Conflict'.* Pope Francis' Ecumenism

ARISTIDE FUMAGALLI: *Journeying in Love.* Pope Francis' Moral Theology

JUAN CARLOS SCANNONE: *The Gospel of Mercy in the Spirit of Discernment.* Pope Francis' Social Ethics

MARINELLA PERRONI: *Kerygma and Prophecy.* Pope Francis' Biblical Hermeneutics

PIERO CODA: *'The Church is the Gospel'.* At the sources of Pope Francis' theology

MARKO IVAN RUPNIK: *According to the Spirit.* Spiritual theology on the move with Pope Francis' Church

ABBREVIATIONS

AG	*Ad Gentes*
CCC	*Catechism of the Catholic Church*
DA	*Document (Aparecida)*
DCE	*Deus Caritas Est*
DM	*Document (Medellín)*
DP	*Document (Puebla)*
EG	*Evangelii Gaudium*
EN	*Evangelii Nuntiandi*
GS	*Gaudium et Spes*
LF	*Lumen Fidei*
LG	*Lumen Gentium*
LS	*Laudato Si'*
MC	*Marialis Cultus*
MeM	*Misericordia et Misera*
MV	*Misericordiae Vultus*
NMI	*Novo Millennio Ineunte*
OA	*Octogesima Adveniens*
RMa	*Redemptoris Mater*
SD	*Document (Santo Domingo)*
SE	*Spiritual Exercises*
UR	*Unitatis Redintegratio*

PREFACE TO THE SERIES

From the time of his first appearance in St Peter's Square on the evening of his election, it was more than clear that Francis' pontificate would be adopting a new style. His modest apparel, calling himself the Bishop of Rome, asking the people to pray for him – in the 'deafening silence' of a packed square – and greeting them with a simple '*buonasera*' (good evening) ... these were all eloquent signs of the fact that there was a change taking place in the way the Pope related to people, and thus in the 'language' used.

The gestures and words that have followed from that occasion only confirm and strengthen this first impression. Indeed, it could be said that over the ensuing years, the image of the papacy has been decidedly transformed, involving a change that affects homilies, addresses and documents promulgated as well.

As could be predicted, this has generated divergent opinions, especially regarding his teaching. While many have in fact welcomed his magisterium with enthusiasm and deep interest, sensing the fresh wind of the gospel, some others have approached it in a more detached way and, at times, with suspicion. There has been no lack of more absolute views, even going as far as to doubt the existence of a theology in Francis' teaching.

A summary judgement of this kind could come from the very different backgrounds of Francis and his predecessor, Benedict XVI. The latter, we know, has been one of the most outstanding and important theologians of the twentieth century and undoubtedly relied on his personal theological development in his rich papal magisterium. We have not yet fully appreciated, nor will we cease to appreciate, the depth of this magisterium. What Bergoglio has behind him, on the other hand, is his long and deep-rooted experience as a religious and a pastor.

However, this does not mean that his magisterium is without a theology. The fact that he was not mostly, or only, a 'professional' theologian does not mean that his magisterium is not supported by a theology. Were this the case, we could say that, strictly speaking, the majority of his predecessors were without a theology, given that Ratzinger represents the exception rather than the rule.

In any case, the fact that we can discuss the theological significance of Francis' magisterium, as well as the fact that, very often, some of his highly evocative and very immediate expressions have been so abused as to rob them of their profundity – in the journalistic as well as the ecclesial ambit – makes the response of this series, which I have the honour of presenting, a significant one.

By drawing on the competence and rigorous study of theologians of proven worth, coming from diverse contexts, the series has sought to research the theological thinking which supports the Pope's teaching. It explores its roots, its freshness, and its continuity with earlier magisterium.

The result can be found in the eleven volumes which make up this series with its simple and direct title: 'The Theology of Pope Francis'.

They can be read independently of one another, obviously; they have been written by individual authors independently of each other. Nevertheless, the hope is that a reading of the entire series would not only be a valuable aid for grasping the theology upon which Francis' teaching is based, in the various theological fields of knowledge, but also an introduction to the key points of his thinking and teaching overall.

The intention, then, is not one of 'apologetics', and even less so is it to add further voices to the many already speaking about the Pope. The aim is to try to see, and to help others to see, what theological thinking Francis bases himself on and expresses, in such a fresh way in his teaching.

Among the many discoveries the reader could make in reading these volumes, would certainly be that of observing how so much of the beneficial freshness of the Council's teaching flows into Francis' magisterium. This is true both of the theological preparation he has had, and of what has followed from it. Given that it is perhaps still too soon for all this wealth to become common patrimony, peacefully and fully received by everyone, it should be no surprise that the Pope's teaching is sometimes not immediately understood by everyone.

By the same token, a point of no return has been reached in Francis' teaching, one that recent theology and the Council have both taught: that doctrine cannot be something extraneous to so-called pastoral theology and ministry. The truth that the Church is called to watch over is the truth of Christ's gospel, which needs to be communicated to the women and men of every time and place. This is why the task of the ecclesial magisterium must also be one of favouring this communication of the gospel. Hence, theology can never be reduced to a dry, desk-bound exercise, disconnected from the life of the people of God and its mission. This mission is that the women and men of every age encounter the perennial and inexhaustible freshness of Jesus' gospel.

Over these years there have been those who have heard some of Francis' own critical statements regarding theology or theologians, and have concluded that he holds it and them in low esteem. Perhaps a more detailed study of the Pope's teaching, such as offered by this series, could also be helpful for showing that, while we always need to be critical of a theology that loses its vital connection to the living faith of the Church, it is also essential to have a theology which takes up the task of thinking critically about this very faith, and doing so with 'creative fidelity', so that it may continue to be proclaimed.

Francis' teaching is certainly not lacking in a theology of this kind; and a theology of the kind is certainly one much desired by a magisterium such as his, which so wants God's mercy to continue to touch the minds and hearts of the women and men of our time.

Editor-in-chief
ROBERTO REPOLE

CONTENTS

Abbreviations 4
Preface to the Series 5
Introduction 13

Chapter 1

FROM MARIAN PIETY TO MARIOLOGY 17

1. *She is my mother: Bergoglio's devotion and Francis' teaching* 17
2. Sensus fidei, *popular spirituality, Marian piety* 20
3. *The faithful people teach us to love Mary.* 23
4. *Mary in connection with the mysteries* 29

Chapter 2

A NOVELTY OF POPE FRANCIS' PONTIFICATE 37

1. *Name and the periphery; a Pope from the South* 37
2. *Popular Latin American Marian spirituality* 43
3. *Looking at the Virgin and placing himself beneath her tender gaze.* 49
4. *Mary in Aparecida and Aparecida in Francis* 56

Chapter 3

Jesus Christ and Mary 65

1. *The novelty and joy of Jesus Christ* 65
2. *The song of the Magnificat: 'My spirit rejoices in God my Saviour'* 69
3. *Mary as believer, disciple and missionary of the gospel* 74
4. *The revolution of tenderness: 'Through the loving mercy of our God'* 83

Chapter 4

Mary and the people of God 89

1. *The pilgrim and evangelizing people of God.* 89
2. *Mary's motherhood and the maternal dimension of the Church* 93
3. *The feminine correlation between Mary, the Church and the faithful Christian* ... 101
4. *Mary precedes, accompanies and protects the pilgrim people* 108

Chapter 5

Mary and the people of the World 115

1. *The conversion or missionary reform of the Church from the periphery* 115
2. *Poor and for the poor. 'He looks on his servant in her lowliness... he raises the lowly'* 120

3. La Morenita: *Our Lady of Guadalupe and the peoples of America* 125
4. Salve Regina, mater misericordiae: *the style of Marian tenderness*.................... 130

INTRODUCTION

μακαριοῦσίν με πᾶσαι αἱ γενεαί (Lk 1: 48b)

Our peoples… find God's affection and love in the face of Mary (*Aparecida* 265).

Whenever we look to Mary, we come to believe once again in the revolutionary nature of love and tenderness (*EG* 288)

Pope Francis is passing on to the Church a spirituality, a pastoral approach and a theology, all focused on the revolution of God's tenderness, of the Father rich in mercy, made manifest in the face of Christ who died and rose again. This tenderness is communicated in the gift of the Holy Spirit. We can read his love for the Virgin Mary, Mother of God, and his teaching about Mary, in this context. The novelty of the first Latin American Pope is expressed in the combination of his figure and his ministry, also in his prayers, words and gestures of a Marian kind. What stands out in his magisterium is the agenda-setting Exhortation *Evangelii Gaudium* (*EG*),[1]

---

1 The Church's documents are cited with the following abbreviations: *Lumen Gentium* (LG), *Gaudium et Spes* (GS), *Marialis Cultus* (MC), *Evangelii Nuntiandi* (EN), *Redemptoris Mater* (RMa), *Catechism of the Catholic Church* (CCC), *Novo Millennio Ineunte* (NMI), *Deus Caritas Est* (DCE), *Lumen Fidei*

an original document which picks up the best of our pastoral theology.[2]

In a conversation I had with him six months after beginning his Petrine service, I presented him with the outline of a book on his thinking and the Latin American Church, which I never completed. He told me then that he was *only a link in a longer chain*, or, *a bead in a longer rosary*. We note this, especially in his Marian spirituality which shares in the faith and piety of the people of God as experienced in Latin America in a particular way. The Pope comes from a land and a history which bring Mary's words into the present: 'all generations will call me blessed' (Lk 1:48b). This missionary and reforming pontificate, which confirms us in joy and faith, finds its roots both in the exceptional figure of Jesuit Jorge Mario Bergoglio and in his belonging to the Latin American Church, and in the part he played in the missionary project of the Fifth General Conference of the Latin American and Caribbean Bishops at Aparecida (*DA*) in 2007. Also, in his mutual understanding of, and feeling for, the various directions of the incipient but promising Argentinian theological reflection.

The current Pope was formed in our country as *a missionary pastor and lucid pastoral thinker*. Over the years,

---

(LF), *Evangelii Gaudium* (EG), *Laudato si'* (LS), *Misericordiae Vultus* (MV), *Misericordia et Misera* (MM), *Documents from Medellín* (DM), *The Puebla Document* (DP), *The Santo Domingo Document* (SD), *The Aparecida Document* (DA). ST refers to the *Summa Theologiae* of St Thomas Aquinas.

2 Cf. CM GALLI, 'La teología pastoral de Aparecida, una de las raíces latinoamericanas de la exhortación Evangelii gaudium', *Gregorianum* 96 (2015) pp. 25–50.

he was a spiritual director and gave courses in spiritual theology and Ignatian spirituality. When he was Rector of the Jesuit Colegio Máximo (1979–1985) he founded and was the first parish priest of the Patriarch St Joseph Parish in the San Miguel neighbourhood in greater Buenos Aires where he gave life to a widespread and active evangelization in the suburbs. At this time he taught Pastoral Theology and commented on Paul VI's Exhortation *Evangelii Nuntiandi* at the Jesuit Theological Faculty in Argentina. Pastoral Theology and Church History (which St John XXIII taught) are disciplines of the one theological science which is speculative and practical (*ST* 1,1, 4).

I will attempt to understand and summarize the Mariology that emerges from the spirituality and pastoral approach of Francis, *by letting his texts speak*. My subtitle highlights the fact that his outlook on Mary is ultimately connected with the mystery of God in Christ, the Church and its mission, the faith of the peoples, especially those in Latin America. I will try to theologically interpret his deeds and writings as they relate to one another. This involves analytical study, a hermeneutical reading and an effort to meditate on the material. There are many sources of the Pope's thinking. For example, he is accustomed to quoting Dante. He did this in 2016, speaking about Mary: V*ergine madre, figlia del tuo figlio, umile e alta pié che creatura [Virgin mother, daughter of thy son, lowly and uplifted more than any creature].*[3]

---

3 A Spadaro, 'Le orme di un pastore. Una conversazione con Papa Francisco' [In the footsteps of a pastor. A conversation with

Here, I will choose and comment on texts by Bergoglio/Francis in their original contexts. I will identify and explain some immediate and intermediate sources, as well as explicit and implicit ones. I will locate and analyse texts which he draws from belonging to conciliar, pontifical and episcopal magisterium. I will look for convergences with contemporary theologians and pastoral thinkers, including some from Argentina. This exercise in theological method combines operations of historical understanding and systematic articulation.

This somewhat discursive path will involve various stages: the shift from Marian piety to Mariology through the *sensus fidei*, the sense of faith of the people (1); the novelty of Francis' pontificate in relation to the Latin American Church, Marian spirituality and the Aparecida project (2); the integration of the mystery of Mary within the mystery of Christ and the proclamation of the gospel (3); the correlation between Mary's motherhood and the Church as Mother, the evangelizing people of God (4); the presence of the Mother of Mercy in the history of the holy people, who live among the peoples of the world (5).

Pope Francis], in: JORGE MARIO BERGOGLIO – PAPA FRANCESCO, *Nei tuoi occhi é la mia parola. Omelie e discorsi di Buenos Aires 1999–2013* [In your eyes is my word. Homilies and addresses from Buenos Aires 1999-2013] , Milan, Rizzoli, 2016, XX.

Chapter 1
FROM MARIAN PIETY TO MARIOLOGY

1. *She is my mother: Bergoglio's devotion and Francis' teaching*

Taking a look at Francis' pontificate, and interpreting his spirituality, pastoral approach and theology in a Marian key, is an exercise in gospel discernment. The Pope's affectionate gestures in the presence of the Virgin – prayers, kisses, embrace – demonstrate this filial love for the Mother of the Lord. At his first public appearance and in the dialogue with the people of his new diocese, Francis invited them to pray the *Hail Mary*, the most popular Marian prayer. On the following day he made a pilgrimage to the Basilica of St Mary Major, the place of the first church dedicated to Our Lady in the West (432–439), where St Ignatius of Loyola celebrated his first Mass on Christmas night (1538). Francis entrusted his ministry to her and left flowers at the foot of the Byzantine icon known as *Salus populi romani*, a supplication to protect the people of Rome.

Mary, faith, mission and the poor are some of the treasures of the Latin American and Caribbean Church. The Pope's piety shares the love for the Virgin which identifies the people of God among us. This feature is noted in his quote from the *Nican Mopohua* account, and in his invitation to contemplate Our Lady of Guadalupe (*EG* 286). In

Mexico, in 2016, he placed himself beneath the gaze of *La Morenita* [a reference to her brown-coloured skin in that representation of the Virgin].

The Pope gives testimony to both the universal value and the inculturated figure of the Blessed Virgin. Regarding the first aspect it suffices to recall the teaching of Blessed Paul IV: 'When the Church considers the long history of Marian devotion she rejoices at the continuity of the element of cult which it shows but she does not bind herself to any particular expression of an individual cultural epoch' (*MC* 36). Bearing this caution in mind, the second perspective is developed in the most complete cultural history of Mariology we have. Stefano de Fiores shows that Mary's image, starting from the outline we find in the Gospel and the truth of faith, has been and is being inculturated in many different cultures of the world.[1]

Brazilian priest, Alexandre Awi Mello, knew Bergoglio at Aparecida and was one of the secretaries of the Editorial Commission. In 2013 he met the Pope once more, and after two extensive interviews and careful investigations, wrote a book on him and the Virgin. His work shows how Francis lives his Marian piety in harmony with the faith of the people of God and thinks of a Mariology 'applied to the life and experience of faith of the people, an authentic and theologically-based popular Marian spirituality.'[2] He tells of

---

1 Cf. S DE FIORES, *María, síntesis de valores. Historia cultural de la mariología*, Madrid, San Pablo, 2011, pp. 731–744.

2 Cf. A AWI MELLO, *Ella es mi mamá. Encuentros del Papa Francisco con María* [She is my mother. Pope Francis' encounters with Mary], Buenos Aires , Patris, 2014, p. 23.

the Pope's prayerful encounters with Mary, which helps him in his ongoing encounter with Jesus, because the encounter of God with human beings is given through her. He describes Bergoglio's Marian piety during different stages of his life. I will take contributions from his study here as a firm basis for attempting a Mariological meditation.

The current Pope's devotion to the Blessed Virgin began in the family, where he learned to pray the three Hail Marys. As a small boy he shared religious practices like the processions to the Basilica of Mary Help of Christians on 24 May; prayer during the enthronement of her image; the blessing of Mary Help of Christians with the prayer *Sub tuum praesidium*.[3] He learned to pray the rosary in the family and Salesian school, which leads him to say: *I am a daily rosary person and the rosary does me good*. In his youth and early adulthood he assimilated devotions via a range of titles and images: Our Lady of Mercy, Our Lady of Pompei, *Stella Maris*, *Salus populi romani*, *Madonna della Strada* [Our Lady of the Way], Mary undoer of knots, Our Lady of Lujan, Our Lady of Guadalupe, the Immaculate Conception of Aparecida, Our Lady of Tenderness… These are many of the titles for just one person, many names for just one mother. She has many faces. At the Casa Santa Marta, Francis has images of Our Lady of Tenderness, Lujan, Miracles …

Marian spiritual experience nurtures the Pope's Petrine ministry and pastoral teaching. When he was Archbishop of Buenos Aires, he preached on the Virgin during the youth

---

3   Cf. A Léon, *Francisco y Don Bosco*, Quito, Publicaciones Pastorales, 2014, pp. 17–67.

pilgrimage to Lujan.⁴ Now he is developing an *ongoing magisterium* focused on the gospel and evangelization, with a strong kerygmatic emphasis, starting with the hierarchy of the truths of faith and virtues organized around charity (*EG* 37).⁵ His teaching concerning the Virgin is expressed in the languages of prayer, homily, speeches, messages. Reprints of his many Marian texts have been published, ordered chronologically or thematically, during a liturgical period or throughout his papacy.⁶

Nevertheless, here we will only be analyzing some selected texts which seem to be central to his Mariology.

2. Sensus fidei, *popular spirituality, Marian piety.*

When *Evangelii Gaudium* refers to Catholic popular piety, it quotes the *Aparecida Document* in six of its notes (nos 98, 102, 103, 104, 106, 107). No. 124 speaks of the 'riches' described in this Document on 'the people's mysticism' (*DA* 258–265). Bergoglio saw to the drafting of this section

---

4 BERGOGLIO preached on the Virgin at Masses celebrated in Lujan in 1999, 2000, 2001, 2004, 2005, 2006, 2008, 2009, 2010, 2011, 2012. There is an incomplete Argentinian edition and another in Italian, complete. The former presents all the texts together (Cf. *El verdadero poder es el servicio* [True power is service], Buenos Aires, Claretiana, 2013, 131–154); the latter locates them with texts written each year (Cf. *Nei tuoi occhi é la mia parola*, pp. 39, 83, 317, 385, 478, 671, 731, 801, 885, 991).

5 Cf. S DIANICH, *Magistero in movimento. Il caso papa Francesco* [The Magisterium on the move. The case of Pope Francis], Bologna, EDB, 2016, pp.15–33.

6 Cf. FRANCESCO, *Maria, aurora del mondo*, Citta del Vaticano, LEV, 2016; M PARDOS RUESCA, *María Madre y Francisco Papa*, Madrid, Cobel-EV, 2016 (a very complete selection of texts up to 2016).

in which at least five Argentinians played a part. He commented on it in 2008 in a work produced by CELAM.[7]

The Latin American reassessment of popular piety began after the Medellín Bishops Conference (1968) and found an echo in a valuable text of Paul VI's (*EN* 48) which, in turn, influenced the Latin American Church as it came to a mature reflection at Puebla. The theology of Lucio Gera, an Argentinian, played a dominant role on the path to Puebla, especially beginning with the paper he delivered, 'People, the people's religion and the Church,'[8] in 1976 at a CELAM meeting, which culminated in the document 'Church and popular religiosity in Latin America.'[9] This symposium re-assessed popular religion and recovered Guadalupan devotion. In 1979 the chapter on *evangelization and popular religion* at Puebla (*DP* 444–469) became a classic on this theme, which was then quoted by the *Catechism of the Catholic Church* (*CCC* 1674–1676) and the *Directory on Popular Piety and Liturgy*. Puebla laid the foundations for recognizing the ecclesiality of the faithful people, because popular Catholic piety is the most significant and numerous of the religious expressions in Latin America.

This theology collaborated in re-assessing popular piety as '*an expression of inculturated Catholic faith*' (*DP* 444).

---

[7] Cf. JM BERGOGLIO, 'La religiosidad popular como inculturación de la fe', in: CELAM - SECRETARÍA GENERAL, *Testigos de Aparecida*, II, Bogotá, CELAM, 2008, pp. 281–325.

[8] Cf. L GERA, *La religione del popolo. Chiesa, teologia e liberazione in America Latina*, Bologna, EDB, 2015.

[9] Cf. CELAM, *Iglesia y Religiosidad Popular en América Latina*, Bogotá, CELAM, 1977.

There is a hermeneutical circle in Latin America between the notion of people of God and popular piety, a religiosity which is manifested, for example, in requesting and celebrating baptism, or making pilgrimages to shrines. Popular piety expresses a living experience of the people of God and this biblical and conciliar concept throws an ecclesiological light on it. This conviction drives a theology which deals with taking up the *sensus fidei fidelium* of the Christian people, which plays a key role in the Latin American reinterpretation of the Second Vatican Council's doctrine. The religious expression of the Catholic Faith is a sign of the belonging of the simple Christian people to God's Church.

Francis' theology of popular piety begins from an ecclesiology which thinks of the relationship between Church and world as an admirable exchange between the people of God and the cultures of the peoples (*GS* 44, *AG* 22).[10] Popular piety presents as the peculiar way the Christian and Catholic people live their faith in the setting of a specific cultural mode.

> Each portion of the people of God, by translating the gift of God into its own life and in accordance with its own genius, bears witness to the faith it has received, and enriches it with new and eloquent expressions. One can say

---

10 Cf. CM GALLI, 'La fuerza evangelizadora de la piedad católica popular in la exhortación *Evangelii gaudium*' [The evangelizing power of popular Catholic piety in the Exhortation *Evangelii Gaudium*], *Phase* 54 (2014) pp. 269–298.

> that 'a people continuously evangelizes itself' (*DP* 450; A 264). Herein lies the importance of popular piety, a true expression of the spontaneous missionary activity of the people of God. This is an ongoing and developing process of which the Holy Spirit is the principal agent (*EG* 122).

With his theology of pastoral ministry for the people, the Pope is affirming the missionary potential of the poor and baptised people as key players in the new evangelization. As the Puebla Conference said, the people's faith as piety is 'an actively evangelizing strength' (*DP* 396). In it is recognised 'a powerful confession of the living God who acts in history, and a channel for handing on the faith' (*DA* 264).

> Underlying popular piety, as a fruit of the inculturated Gospel, is an active evangelizing power which we must not underestimate: to do so would be to fail to recognize the work of the Holy Spirit. Instead, we are called to promote and strengthen it, in order to deepen the never-ending process of inculturation (*EG* 126).

3. *The faithful people teach us to love Mary.*

Francis values popular Christianity as 'a channel for handing on the faith' (*DA* 264). The people of God hand on the faith in many different ways, among them delicate, informal person-to-person communication (*EG* 127–129). 'Being a disciple means being constantly ready to bring the love of Jesus to others, and this can happen unexpectedly and in any place: on the street, in a city square, during work, on a journey' (*EG* 127). The faith of the Christian faithful is like a call or rather, as Jesuit and Chilean Saint Alberto Hurtado would say, like 'a fire that sparks other fires.'

The Argentinian Pope considers popular piety to be a *theological place* for thinking about faith and mission: 'Expressions of popular piety have much to teach us; for those who are capable of reading them, they are a *locus theologicus* which demands our attention, especially at a time when we are looking to the new evangelization' (*EG* 126). These expressions teach us much about Mary.

Father Jorge Mario Bergoglio was presenting the teaching of the Council on the *sensus fidei fidelium* and the *in credendo* infallibility of the holy people of God (*LG* 12a) since 1974. He has indicated that just as the magisterium and theology faithfully present the *content* of what we believe, for example, concerning Mary as the Mother of God, popular piety manifests, in living form, how the Church believes in and loves the Virgin Mary.[11] In his agenda-setting Exhortation, Francis confirms this truth about the vital wisdom of the faith of the community of all the baptised (*EG* 119). He learned love for the Virgin from the witness, prayer and words of his grandmother Rosa, the woman who made the greatest impression on his life and who grew up in the Piedmontese Catholic culture at the height of the 'Marian era' of the 19th century. In her will and testament she

---

11 Cf. JM BERGOGLIO, *Meditaciones para religiosos*, Buenos Aires, Ediciones Diego de Torres, 1982, p. 47.

addressed to her grandchildren, she wrote that in difficult moments 'a glance at Mary at the foot of the cross can make a drop of soothing balm fall on the deepest and most painful of wounds.'[12] Thus the Pope learned to look at and love the Virgin in an inculturated way.

The holy people teach all their members, including those called to the ordained ministry. In 2011, Pope Benedict XVI highlighted the hidden treasure there is in our Latin American popular religion. It showed its vital sense of belonging to the Church, and he said that it 'sees that we ourselves (the clergy) are fully integrated within the people of God.'[13]

Theological reflection on Mary takes root in the *sensus fidei fidelium*, which recognises her as the Mother of God. The faith of the people of God is a simple faith, which bears within it a theology that does not err, because the Spirit of God is in it. The Pope quotes Vatican II's Constitution *Lumen Gentium* frequently, where it says: 'the holy people of God cannot err in matters of belief' (*LG* 12a).

Asked about the significance of 'thinking with the Church,' the Bishop of Rome replied:

> Thinking with the Church, therefore, is my way of being a part of this people. And all the faithful, considered as a whole, are infallible in matters of

---

12   L Capuzzi, *Rosa de los dos mundos. La historia de la abuela del Papa Francisco*, Madrid, Palabra, 2015, 19.

13   Benedict XVI, 'Piedad popular y nueva evangelización', in: Pontificia Comisión para América Latina, *La piedad popular en el proceso de evangelización de América Latina*, p. 15.

> belief, and the people display this *infallibilitas in credendo*, this infallibility in believing, through a supernatural sense of the faith of all the people walking together. This is what I understand today of the 'thinking with the Church' of which St Ignatius speaks. When the dialogue among the people and the bishops and the pope goes down this road and is genuine, then it is assisted by the Holy Spirit. So this thinking with the Church does not concern theologians only.
>
> This is how it is with Mary: if you want to know who she is ask theologians; if you want to know how to love her, you have to ask the people. In turn, Mary loved Jesus with the heart of the people, as we read in the Magnificat. We should not even think, therefore, that 'thinking with the Church' means only thinking with the hierarchy of the Church.[14]

Love for the people implies knowing, valuing and learning from the people's embodied faith and filial love. This is why an inculturated theology must begin with faith embodied in piety, devotion, which in turn is the result of an historical and culturally contextualized evangelization. In this case it was a Marian catechesis communicated in the first evangelization of America from California to Chile, by

---

14 A. SPADARO, 'Intervista a Papa Francisco' [Interview with Pope Francis. This interview is available in English at www.americamagazine.org/faith/2013/09/30/big-heart-open-god-interview-pope-francis], *La Civiltá Cattolica* 3918 (2013) p. 459.

means of catechisms and devotional books in Spanish and indigenous languages.[15] Cardinal Bergoglio stated this in 2012 when he presented a study on the theology of the faith by Argentinian theologian and pastoral thinker Rafael Tello, in the same year in which he sought to have the remains of Lucio Gera, another great Argentinian theologian and pastoral thinker, brought to the crypt of the Cathedral in Buenos Aires.

> It is good – and necessary – for theology to be concerned with popular devotion. It is the 'precious treasure of the Catholic church in Latin America' Benedict XVI told us at the opening of the Aparecida Conference. Father Tello offers a solid theological thinking which we can value in order to appreciate this spirituality in its true dimension.[16]

Essays are written in Latin America on Marian history, theology, pastoral ministry and spirituality, starting from the love for Mary which has made its home at the heart of popular Catholic Christianity. There are studies which analyze and summarize the theological context of these representations of Marian devotion expressed in events,

---

15 Cf. J Durán, 'Resonancias marianas en los catecismos hispanoamericanos del siglo XVI', en: *Monumenta Catechetica Hispanoamericana. Siglos XVI–XVIII*. III, Buenos Aires, Agape, 2017, pp. 847–927.

16 JM Bergoglio – Francisco, 'Prefazione', in: E Bianchi, *Introduzione alla teologia del popolo. Profilo spirituale e teológico di Rafael Tello*, Bologna, Emi, 2015, p. 18.

images, patronal feasts, and national shrines[17] along with the religious, symbolic, artistic, literary, cultural and social forms accompanying them. Standing out is the integrating hermeneutic of the image and account of Our Lady of Guadalupe.[18] Gradually, a rich inculturated Mariology is being written and spoken, which picks up and thinks of the mystery of the Mother of God, beginning with historical expressions of Marian piety.[19]

An inculturated theology seeks to concretize the challenge launched by the Second Vatican Council when asking local Churches to investigate 'by what paths faith and intelligence can arrive, taking into consideration philosophy or the wisdom of the peoples' (*AG* 22b). A hermeneutic of the representations of popular faith in God, Christ, the Eucharist, Mary and the Church enriches the understanding of these mysteries and helps to advance along the path of inculturation. Theological know-how should take root in the theological wisdom of the people of God which is alive in different cultures and seeks an inculturated understanding

17   Cf. CELAM, *Nuestra Señora de América* I–II, Bogotá, CELAM, 1988.

18   Cf. J GUERRERO, *El Nican Mopohua. Un intento de exégesis* I–II, México, Realidad Teoría y Práctica, 1998; J. GUERRERO; F. GONZÁLEZ; E. CHAVEZ; *El encuentro de la Virgen de Guadalupe y Juan Diego*, México, Porrúa, 2001.

19   Cf. M SILVEIRA, *Mariología popular latinoamericana. Fisonomía de la mariología popular venezolana*, Caracas, Universidad Católica Andrés Bello, 2013; M TEMPORELLI, *María, mujer de Dios y de los pobres. Relectura de los dogmas marianos*, Buenos Aires, San Pablo, 2008; A GONZÁLEZ DORADO, *De la María conquistadora a la María liberadora. Ensayo de mariología popular latinoamericana*, Santander, Sal Terrae, 1988.

of the faith. In 1996, at a meeting called by the *Latin American Episcopal Council* and the *Congregation for the doctrine of the faith*, presided over by Cardinal Ratzinger, the sixteen participants subscribed to the following proposition: 'we need to pursue the path of inculturation of theological reflection so that it is fully Catholic and fully Latin American.[20]

4. *Mary in connection with the mysteries*

The Christian Faith has as its object the mystery of the Triune God and his plan of salvation. But its contents are mysteries and the mysteries are persons: the Three Divine Persons in the identity of the one God; the person of Jesus Christ, God and man; the person of Mary, Mother of God; the Church as a communion of persons; the saints in heaven; pilgrims on earth. Faith is made up of personal encounters. The popes employ this category to tell of the believing experience and focus on the encounter with Christ (*Ecclesia in America* 8–12, *DCE* 1).

Aparecida indicates that Jesus attracts people to himself and presents evangelization as attraction, beginning with the gift of the encounter with Christ (*DA* 12, 159, 268, 274, 277). It takes up this category when it presents popular spirituality as a way to encounter with Christ (*DA* 263). Francis refers to faith as a personal encounter with the Lord (*EG*) and, besides, promotes 'the culture of encounter' among the peoples (*EG* 220).

20 CELAM, *El futuro de la reflexión teológica en América Latina*, Bogotá, Documentos CELAM pp. 141,1996, 367.

Mary expresses the connection of the mysteries among themselves (*nexus mysteriosum inter se*) and is an icon which condenses the mystery, a fragment which reproduces the whole. She is in the heart of Christ and the Church. Chapter 8 of *Lumen Gentium* is entitled: *The Blessed Virgin Mary, Mother of God, in the mystery of Christ and the Church* (*LG* 52–59). For Joseph Ratzinger, the inclusion of Mariology in ecclesiology was no casual decision, but corresponds to the main thread running through this Constitution. For the Council Fathers 'the Church is anticipated in Mary, it is in the person of Mary… and Mary carries within herself the total mystery of the Church.'[21] There is reciprocity between both. Paul VI's Mariology takes the same position in his Exhortation *Marialis Cultus* (*MC*) as does John Paul II in the Encyclical *Redemptoris Mater* (*RMa*). Between both of these texts, the *Puebla Document*, coming from the Third General Conference of the Latin American and Caribbean Bishops (1979), presented Mary in relation to truths about Christ, the Church and man (*DP* 282–303).

In continuity with the Council, John Paul II made an excellent summary regarding Mary in the light of the mysteries of Christ and the Church (*RMa* 4). He structured his Encyclical according to this principle by entitling his chapters: Mary in Christ (*RMa* 7–24), in the Church (*RMa* 25–37), in Christ and the Church (*RMa* 38–50). Hence we contemplate Mary from Christ and the Church:

---

21 J RATZINGER, 'Eclesiología de la Constitución *Lumen gentium*', in: *Obras completas* VIII/1: *Iglesia, signo entre los pueblos*, Madrid, BAC, 2015, p. 560.

'Mary belongs indissolubly to the mystery of Christ, and she belongs also to the mystery of the Church from the beginning' (*RMa* 27). On the other hand, the opposite and complementary perspective is also true. Following Paul VI, the Polish Pope stated that 'Mary will always be key to the exact understanding of the mystery of Christ and of the Church' (*RMa* 47). Hence, we also need to contemplate Christ and the Church from Mary, from her faith. 'Blessed is she who believed' (Lk 1:45). She is the 'first of the believers' (*RMa* 26). She began 'her whole pilgrimage of faith' (*RMa* 14) with the Annunciation. John Paul II developed this aspect in a very original way (*RMa* 12–19) and consistently showed that the Virgin's faith 'continues to become the faith of the pilgrim People of God' (*RMa* 28)[22]

Renewed contemporary Mariology explains the truth about Mary in connection with theology involving God, Christ, the Church and the human being.[23] For example, it understands the titles 'Virgin', 'Bride' and 'Mother' by relating their theological, ecclesiological and anthropological meanings.[24] In particular, theology contemplates and thinks of Mary in relation to Christ and his Church, and also looks

---

22 Cf. JOHANNES PAUL II, *Maria – Gottes Ja zum Menschen. Enzyklika Mutter des Erlösers*, Freiburg, Herder, 1987. The introduction by J. Ratzinger and commentary by H.U. von Balthasar highlight Mary's faith (Cf. 116–118 & 133–136). This point is central to the Mariology of both theologians, Cf. *Maria – Chiesa nascente*, Rome, Paoline, 1981.

23 Cf. P LARGO, 'Panorama mariológico-mariano de la primera década del siglo XXI', *Marianum* 189 (2016) pp. 381–489.

24 Cf. B FORTE, *María, la mujer icono del misterio*, Salamanca, Sigueme, 1993, pp. 179–275.

at Christ and the Church through the eyes of Mary's faith. Glorified, she is 'The image and beginning of the Church as it is to be perfected in the world to come' (*LG* 68). Recent Mariology, in accordance with the patristic tradition, focuses on the correlation that exists between Mary and the Church.[25]

The confession of faith in Jesus Christ, *vere Deus* and *vere homo*, is the foundation for the Catholic affirmation of concrete humanity's active participation in the economy of salvation, whereas Lutheran theology has tended to speak of God's action 'in' humanity, and has therefore run the risk of shifting 'from God's Omnipotence (*Allvirksamkeit Gottes*) to God's exclusive action (*Alleinwirksamkeit Gottes*).'[26] The Saviour of the world is 'Christ Jesus, himself human' (I Tim 2:5) the 'one mediator between God and humankind.' His holy humanness is 'the universal cause of salvation' (*ST III, 4, 4, ad 1um*; *III, 26, 2 ad 3um*) and the foundation of human cooperation is God's work. By contrast with *soli Deo* and *opus Dei soli*, Catholic doctrine maintains that along with the primacy of grace, the human being can cooperate with the action of the one Mediator, in and under grace. In an essay marking one of the centenaries of the Council of Chalcedon, Yves Congar said that 'Catholic statements concerning our three themes – the Church, Mary, Christ –

---

25 Cf. G GRESHAKE, *Maria – Ecclesia. Prospettive di una teologia e una prassi ecclesiale fondata in senso mariano*, Brescia, Queriniana, 2017, pp. 133–161, 373–429, 430–443, 453–464.

26 B SESBOÜE, "Ya-t-il une différence séparatrice entre les ecclésiologies catholique et protestante?", *Nouvelle Revue Théologique* 109 (1987) pp.3–30, 23.

are connected with one another and depend on a principle that can be applied, *positis ponendis*, in the three cases: humankind's cooperation in the work of salvation, the virtue of which clearly comes from God.'[27]

This principle of cooperation includes the contributions of individuals and communities in the one inclusive and universal mediation of Jesus Christ, and grounds the mission of passing on the gospel 'from person to person.' The dignity God has given the human being makes it possible to freely cooperate with his work. This principle is realised differently in Jesus, Mary and the Church, and in human beings. In the redemptive Incarnation, Mary's 'yes' represents human and ecclesial cooperation in divine behaviour. John Paul II included the mediation, cooperation or motherly intercession of Mary in the unique and inclusive meditation of Christ (*RMa* 40), as a 'shared cooperation' (*RMa* 38).

Jesus Christ is the centre of history and of faith, a centred and centering centre in the Father through the Love of the Spirit. In Christ, God-Man and Man-God, *the Triune God is at the centre* because Christ is centred on the Father, to whom he is eternally united in the Spirit. Trinitarian Christocentrism keeps the balance between Christological concentration and Trinitarian overflow.

In Christ *human beings too, are at the centre* because he is the divine and eschatological model of the human being, who 'reveals man to man himself' (*GS* 22). Christ makes manifest the concrete human being as revealed by

27 Y CONGAR, *Cristo, María y la Iglesia*, Barcelona, Estela, 1964, 30; cf. pp. 19–20, 29, 36–38, 44, 49–52, 70.

God and contemplated in a christocentric and trinitarian anthropology. The Council highlighted this bipolarity within christocentrism (*GS* 24, 32, 41). In 1967, with that teaching of the Council as background, Paul VI described the theology of Saint Francis de Sales – and all Catholic theology – as christocentric super-humanism (*superhumanismus christocentricus*).[28]

In Christ, the Centre, *Mary is also at the centre*. Christ gives us to Mary, his Mother, as our Mother, and Mary leads us to Christ, her Son. She is not the centre, but through freely given divine love she is and will always be at the centre of history and of faith. One value of popular Catholic wisdom needing, like all the Church, to be 'evangelized ever anew' (*DP* 457), is its tendency to vital synthesis, because 'it joins the divine and the human' as the Puebla Document said (*DP* 448). The religion of the people goes from Mary to Christ and from Christ to Mary. Tello, whom Bergoglio called 'the theologian of the Virgin', stressed this union because it saw 'the Virgin as a saving unity with Christ, constituting an *unum* with Him.'[29] We must not separate what God has united. We go 'through Christ to Mary' because God wanted a Mother for his Son, and we go 'to Christ through Mary' because the Mother always leads to the Son (Jn 2:5).

---

28   PAUL VI, Apostolic Letter 'Sabaudiae Gemma', *Acta Apostolicae Sedis* 59 (1967) 118.
29   R TELLO, *La nueva evangelización* I, Buenos Aires, Agape - Saracho, 2008, 77; cf. pp. 26–32.

Francis situates himself within the tradition of the faith of the people of God and in continuity with the magisterium of the Council and of his predecessors. He confirms his brothers in the faith with the charism that Jesus gave Peter, (Lk 22: 32). He contemplates the divine mercy in the mirror of Mary and reads a summary of the gospel in her. Along with the Christian people, 'in her he "reads" all the truths transmitted by God and taken up by the Church in the Creed.'[30] He looks at the woman praying and working at Nazareth, presents the Church as a woman, and considers the key role of women. He begins from spiritual and pastoral experience which is the cradle of wise theological thinking. He contributes a theologically-based, popular Marian spirituality, and a wise theology which spontaneously combines theology with spirituality and pastoral ministry, especially through the homily and catechesis. The tender gaze the Virgin casts on us illumines believing contemplation and nurtures theological reflection on Mary. This is the key to a Mariology informed by wisdom, that is, a theological, prayerful, historical, prophetic and evangelizing Mariology.

---

30 R TELLO, *La nueva evangelización* II, Buenos Aires, Agape, 2013, p. 53.

Chapter 2
A NOVELTY OF POPE FRANCIS' PONTIFICATE

1. *Name and the periphery; a Pope from the South*

Nomen est omen. Name is mission. The first Jesuit Pope chose the name of the *Poverello*. He accepted the recommendation of Cardinal Claudio Hummes who reminded him of what St Paul said: do not forget the poor (Gal 2:10; *EG* 193–196). None of his predecessors before had taken the name Francis. In 2013, during his pilgrimage to Assisi, the Pope recalled Francis' union with Jesus who converted Francis into an *alter Christus*, and his dedication to the mission he received in service of the Church: *repair my house*. The Bishop of Rome presented three salient features of Francis: his love for the poor, by embracing *Lady Poverty*; his charism for peace, encoded in the motto *Peace and good*; his fellowship with creation, expressed in the praise of the *Canticle of Creatures*.[1] For this Pope, Francis is a guiding light. His name has strong prophetic value. It denotes union with Christ for the greater glory of God, salvation of human beings, and missionary renewal of the Church. And

1 Cf. FRANCISCO, 'Homilía en la plaza de San Francisco', *L'Osservatore romano* (weekly edition in Spanish), 11/10/2013, 5. This can be found in English at w2.vatican.va/content/francesco/en/homilies/2013/documents/papa-francesco_20131004_omelia-visita-assisi.html

it offers a symbolic response to three of the dramas affecting humanity today: poverty, peace and creation. From the heart of the gospel of merciful love, Francis presents the social teaching of the Church as a prophecy about justice, peace and looking after our common home.

The Pope presents his program in the Exhortation *Evangelii Gaudium, The Joy of the Gospel,* in which he responds to the request for a document, with contributions from the 2012 Synod on *New evangelization*. He limits himself to just a few issues but develops them so as to 'give shape to a definite style of evangelization which I ask you to adopt in every activity which you undertake' (*EG* 18). The Exhortation is agenda-setting:

> Nevertheless, I want to emphasise that what I am trying to express here has a programmatic significance and important consequences. I hope that all communities will devote the necessary effort to advancing along the path of a pastoral and missionary conversion which cannot leave things as they presently are (*EG* 25).

In accordance with his ministry, name and program, the Exhortation formulates the social dimensions of the gospel and tackles two crucial issues: the poor (*EG* 186–216) and peace (*EG* 217–258). In one paragraph on poor people he invites us to follow Francis' attitude: 'Small yet strong in the love of God, like Saint Francis of Assisi, all of us, as Christians, are called to watch over and protect the fragile world in which we live, and all its peoples' (*EG* 216).

The Encyclical *Laudato Si'* picks up the charism of Saint Francis (*LS* 10–12). He testifies to 'harmony with God, with others, with nature and with himself. He shows us just how inseparable the bond is between concern for nature, justice for the poor, commitment to society, and interior peace' (*LS* 10).

Francis is the first successor of St Peter to come from the southern, Latin American and Argentinian Church. The Holy Spirit 'blows where it chooses' (Jn 3: 8) and has blown like the 'rush of a violent wind' (Acts 2:2). Since 2012 I have been using an image created by Walter Kasper: '*The Wind Blows from the South*.'[2] In 2013, the Spirit of God blew from the ends of the earth. Francis was elected when the outer fringes of the globe appeared at the heart of the globe. He represents the arrival of the Latin American South in the heart of the Church, and as he has shown at the UN and in other forums, he represents the voice of the global South in the world. *With Francis the Latin American Church completes its entry into world history.*

> What the Latin American Church is doing will play an immense role in the Third World... At the same time... Latin America could impact decisively on the destiny of the Church in Europe... Latin America and its

---

2 Cf. W KASPER, *Chiesa Cattolica*, Brescia, Queriniana, 2012, 46 available in English as *The Catholic Church: Nature, Reality and Mission*, Angus and Robertson, 2015; Cf. CM GALLI, 'En la Iglesia está soplando el Viento del Sur', in: CELAM, *Hacia una Nueva Evangelización*, Bogotá, CELAM, 2012, 161–260.

> Church have a great opportunity and I believe that the opportunity for the world Church passes in some way through our Church... The opportunity for renewal of the World Church passes through Latin America and this places a serious responsibility on us.[3]

The Church is growing in the South. The makeup of Catholicism has changed over a period of a century. In 1910, 70% of baptized Catholics lived in the North and 30% in the South. In 2010 just 32% lived in the North (24% in Europe, 8% in North America) and 68% in continents further south (39% in Latin America, 16% in Africa, 12% in Asia, 1% in Oceania). In other words, two out of three are Catholic. The continents with major growth in Catholicism are Africa and Asia. The naming of new cardinals by the Bishop of Rome represents this ecclesial reality proportionately.

After a first millennium marked by the Western Church, we are about to see a third millennium revitalized by the Churches from the South in an intercultural Catholicity, confirmed in the faith and presided over in love by the Roman See, and animated by a *polycentric* dynamic. The third and Southern Church is at the heart of God's house.[4] With the *kairos* of the new pontificate the Catholic Church recognizes the key role of the periphery, and 'the people on the periphery.'[5] The Latin American Church, being on

3 A METHOL FERRÉ, 'Marco histórico de la Iglesia latinoamericana', *SEDOI* 4 (1974) 1–12, esp. 11.

4 Cf. W BÜHLMANN, *La tercera iglesia a las puertas*, Madrid, Paulinas, 2ª, 1977, pp. 157–196.

5 Cf. A RICCARDI, *Periferie. Crisi e novitá per la Chiesa*, Milan,

the periphery, becomes a centre without pretending to be centralized.

In the South, the Catholic Church of Latin America has much history, a huge population, and integration. It has been part of space and time in Latin America since 1492 and has cooperated in forging both the identity of the peoples and the features and appearance of the region. Hence, from its birth it has been involved in serving the formation of an integrated community of nations (*DA* 1–18, 127–128, 50–528). Since 1955, our Church has taken on a new, regional figure. It brings together twenty-one bishops coordinated by CELAM, the Latin American Episcopal Council. This community of Churches on a continental scale carried out a regional, collegial and creative reception of the Second Vatican Council. The process began with the Second Conference at Medellín (1968), which celebrates its fiftieth anniversary in 2018; this was followed, in the light of *Evangelii Nuntiandi*, by the Third at Puebla (1979); it continued with the Fourth at Santo Domingo (1992) in the context of new evangelization proposed by John Paul II.

Jorge Mario Bergoglio has repeatedly expressed his ecclesial, theological, spiritual, emotional, cultural and political belonging to Latin America, his 'beloved continent' (*EG* 124). In various writings he has carried out a hermeneutic of our culture, coming closer to those who 'are encouraged to think of America from America and as Latin Americans.'[6]

Jaca Book, 2016, pp. 7–29.
6 JM Bergoglio, 'Prólogo', in: A Podetti, *Comentario a la Introducción a la 'Fenomenología del Espíritu'*, Buenos Aires, Biblos,

Today, Francis is a symbol of the *Latin American pastoral style:* it is reflected in his closeness to the people, warmth in dealing with people, simplicity in preaching. He brings a simplicity to his life and ministry which leads many people to say: 'The Pope is one of us, one like us.' He takes children in his arms, kisses the sick, greets everyone, blesses each and every one. It is a sign of passing on the faith through a warm, symbolic culture of gesture and celebration which manifests the Latin American and Caribbean style.

The Latin American and Caribbean region is the most urbanized in the world. Eight out of ten people live in urban areas, most in suburban districts. Since 1965, our Church has sought a new urban pastoral ministry (*DA* 509– 519). In my book *Dios vive en la ciudad* (God lives in the city), I show that Bergoglio was the first Archbishop of Buenos Aires formed in our new urban culture.[7] In 1936, when this son of Italian immigrants was born, Buenos Aires already had more than 2,400,000 inhabitants (880,000 foreigners and 1,600,000 locals). He is the first Pope born in a great 20th Century *polis*. This is why he thinks about the tensions between globalization and urbanization, and contemplates the presence of God amid urban cultures and so many 'urban remnants' (*EG* 71–75).[8] One novelty of the current

2007, p. 13.

7 Cf. CM GALLI, *Dio vive in cittá. Verso una nuova pastorale urbana*, Vatican, LEV, 2014, p. 303.

8 Cf. CM GALLI, 'El Pueblo de Dios en las culturas urbanas a la luz de la *Evangelii gaudium*', in: CONSEJO EPISCOPAL LATINOAMERICANO, *Evangelización en las culturas urbanas*, Bogotá, CELAM, 2015, pp. 105–142.

Bishop of Rome is to reflect the Marian face of our regional Church.

2. Popular Latin American Marian spirituality

Catholic Christianity is a key feature of the character of the Latin American and Caribbean Church. The major popular religion in Latin America is a privileged expression of the inculturation of the Catholic Faith. Between Conferences held at Medellín and Puebla de los Angeles, the Church developed a process of theoretical and practical re-evaluation of popular piety and devotion, which was noticed at the Synod in 1974. While the Declaration on Justice in the World in 1971 dealt with the relationship between evangelization, justice and liberation, at the 1974 Assembly on *evangelization*, issues of evangelization of culture, integral liberation, popular religion, made their appearance.

Bishop Eduardo Pironio, the then Bishop of Mar del Plata and President of CELAM, presented the report on evangelization in today's world in Latin America.[9] He set out the *Paschal and Marian face* of our Church, marked by the cross and hope, and stated that the treasure of Latin American popular piety is the departure point for a new evangelization.

---

9 E PIRONIO, *La evangelización de América Latina*, in: CONSEJO EPISCOPAL LATINOAMERICANO, *Evangelización, desafío de la Iglesia. Sínodo de 1974: documentos papales y sinodales. Presencia del CELAM y del Episcopado Latinoamericano*, Bogotá, CELAM, 1976, pp. 113–125; republished in E. PIRONIO, *Signos en la Iglesia latinoamericana*, Buenos Aires, Guadalupe – Faculty of Theology, 2012, pp. 67–92.

The Latin American Church contemplates *the mystical heart of the pilgrim people of God in our peoples*. This theological outlook was indicated by Pironio in 1974, before Puebla. The Argentinian bishop said that 'Latin America was evangelized under the sign of Mary and in the fruitfulness of Christ's cross.'[10] In 2010, almost forty years later, Pope Benedict XVI's outlook merges with that understanding, after Aparecida. The German Pope asserted that 'there are two figures that have made people in Latin America believe; on the one hand the Mother of God and on the other, the God who suffers, who is also suffering in all the violence they themselves have experienced.'[11]

The religious context of the event and the *Aparecida Document* was the prayer taking place at that shrine, a privileged setting for experiencing popular Catholic devotion (*DA* 1–5), a privileged 'expression of the Catholic Faith' (*DA* 258). There, our Church went more deeply into its assessment of popular spirituality, 'the people's mysticism.' (*DA* 258–265). Twice it calls it popular spirituality or mysticism (*DA* 262–263) because it shapes 'a living spiritual experience' (*DA* 259) 'a true experience of theological love' (*DA* 263), 'which delicately permeates the personal existence of each believer, and even the believer lives in a multitude, it is not a 'mass spirituality" (*DA* 261).[12]

---

10 PIRONIO, *La evangelización de América Latina*, in: CELAM, *Evangelización*, p. 116.
11 BENEDICTO XVI, *Luz del mundo. El Papa, la Iglesia y los signos de los tiempos*, Barcelona, Herder, 2010, p. 172.
12 Cf. J SEIBOLD, *La mística popular*, Buena Prensa, Mexico, 2006, p. 196.

We cannot deprecate *popular spirituality*, or consider it a secondary mode of Christian life, for that would be to forget the primacy of the action of the Spirit and God's free initiative of love. *Popular piety* contains and expresses a powerful sense of transcendence, a spontaneous ability to find support in God and a true experience of theological love. It is also an expression of supernatural wisdom, because the wisdom of love does not depend directly on the enlightenment of the mind, but on the internal action of grace. That is why we call it popular spirituality, that is, a Christian spirituality which, while it is a personal encounter with the Lord, includes much of the bodily, the perceptible, the symbolic, and people's most concrete needs. It is a spirituality incarnated in the culture of the lowly, which is not thereby less spiritual, but is no in another manner (*DA* 263).

Popular spirituality is not a residual combination of external and traditional devotions, but a religious expression of the faith of the people of God in a concrete cultural way. The Pope states:

> On that beloved continent, where many Christians express their faith through popular piety, the bishops also refer to it as 'popular spirituality' or 'the people's mysticism.' It is truly 'a spirituality incarnated in the culture of the lowly' (*EG* 124).

Behind the statements of Puebla and Aparecida, there is a way of understanding the relationship between the Christian faith and human religiosity. According to the logic of the Incarnation, by which the Word became one of us, theological faith, a gift of God, and human religion, an expression of spirituality, come together while remaining distinct, and are distinct in coming together. They should not be confused as a mixture, nor be separated by division. They combine so that *faith is expressed in religious terms and religion is theologically inspired by faith.* For Thomas Aquinas 'religion is not faith but the profession of faith (*fides protestatio*) through certain outward signs' (*ST* II–II, 91, *I ad Ium*). This Catholic theology of faith and religion supports the assessment carried out by the Latin American Church.

Aparecida states that popular spirituality is one kind of *personal encounter with the Lord*. There are many expressions of faith, love and devotion in *Christological piety*, which Puebla had already made reference to from Christmas to the Easter Cross (*DP* 448, 454). In his opening address at Aparecida (*DI*), Benedict XVI named a number of them:

- love for the suffering Christ, the God of compassion, pardon and reconciliation: the God who loved us to the point of handing himself over for us.
- love for the Lord present in the Eucharist …
- the God who is close to the poor and to those who suffer' (*DI* 1).

The Pope referred to adoration of the crucified God with expressions which are very much his and which speak to the core of faith: 'God with a human face; he is God-with-us, the God who loves even to the Cross' (*DI* 4).

The Aparecida Document recognises 'the Marian spirit of our popular religiosity which leads to Christ' (*DA* 43). It highlights 'devotion to the suffering Christ and to his Blessed Mother' (*DA* 127). It shows the union between the suffering Lord and his Mother which brings us into a family.

> Our peoples particularly identify with the suffering Christ; they look at him, kiss him, or touch his wounded feet as though saying: This is he 'who has loved me and given himself up for me' (Gal 2: 20). Many of them, beaten, ignored, dispossessed, hold their arms aloft. With their characteristic religiosity, they firmly adhere to the immense love that God has for them, and that continually reminds them of their own dignity. They also find God's affection and love in the face of Mary. In it they see reflected the essential gospel message. From the shrine of Guadalupe our beloved Mother makes her littlest children feel that they are in the fold of her cloak. Now, from Aparecida, she invites them to cast their nets into the world to bring out of anonymity those who are sunk in oblivion, and bring them to the light of faith. Gathering her children, she brings our peoples together around Jesus Christ (*DA* 265).

In the brown face of the *Virgin of Guadalupe*, in the black face of *Our Lady of Aparecida*, in so many images and local, regional, national and continental religious celebrations, we perceive the material love of God made manifest in Christ and Mary to the poorest of the poor. In the faces of original beautiful baroque Latin American images of patient and glorious Christs, such as the Christ of Esquipulas in Guatemala, or the Lord of Miracles in Lima – black, or originating from black archconfraternities – we find symbolized some of the colours of our peoples' *mestizo* and cross-cultural provenance.

'Popular spirituality is *a legitimate way of living the faith*, a way of feeling part of the Church and a way of being missionaries where the deepest vibrations of America's depths come together. It is part of a "cultural historic originality" (*DP* 446) of the poor of this continent, and fruit of a "synthesis between their cultures and Christian faith."' (*DA* 264). This spiritual experience and this sense of belonging has been conceived and accompanied by the Mother of the people of God in our history.

> Since then, countless communities have found in her the closest inspiration for learning how to be disciples and missionaries of Jesus. We joyfully note that she has become part of the journey of each of our peoples, deeply entering into the fabric of their history and taking on the noblest and most significant features of the people in them. The various devotions and shrines spread all over the continent attest to Mary's closeness to the people, and they likewise manifest the faith and trust that her devotees feel toward her.

> She belongs to them and they experience her as
> mother and sister (*DA* 269).

3. *Looking at the Virgin and placing himself beneath her tender gaze.*

Francis' warm gaze, his devotion to and preaching about Mary, find their roots in this fertile soil. Marian shrines in the Latin American Church are places where her children encounter the Father's mercy expressed through Mary's tenderness. Francis teaches:

> As a true mother, she walks at our side, she shares our struggles and she constantly surrounds us with God's love. Through her many titles, often linked to her shrines, Mary shares the history of each people which has received the Gospel and she becomes a part of their historic identity. Many Christian people ask that their children be baptised in a Marian shrine, as a sign of their faith in her motherhood which brings forth new children for God. There, in these many shrines, we can see how Mary brings together her children, who with great effort, come as pilgrims to see her and to be seen by her. Here they find strength from God to bear the weariness and suffering in their lives (*EG* 286).

Luján and Aparecida are two devotions which come from images of the *Immaculate Conception*. This devotion, which took root in Spain and Portugal, was spread by the Franciscans and Jesuits who evangelised parts of our continent, and it marks the style of Latin American Catholicism. The images in both shrines are very small and made of terracotta, almost certainly from the Sao Paulo region of Brazil. In 1992, when Bergoglio was ordained Auxiliary Bishop of Buenos Aires, he began supporting the *Missionary pilgrimage on foot* which left Guadalupe in Mexico in 1992 and arrived at Luján, in Argentina, in 2000. He also began to take part in youth and archdiocesan pilgrimages to the Shrine at Luján, 73 km from the heart of our capital city. Since 1975, this youth pilgrimage has taken place each first Saturday of October, and over more than four decades, has brought millions of Argentinians together. The group departs from the Shrine at San Cayetano in the suburb of Liniers, another place of popular prayer. They walk for some 60 kilometres over 16 hours or more. Pilgrims arrive at Luján on both the Saturday and Sunday. Francis comments:

> We are speaking of a million, a million and a half people, and this is credible because it lasts for practically three days. The first pilgrims leave on Friday night, arrive on Saturday morning at Luján and then return. These pilgrims go in groups or alone. Later the largest group leaves Liniers at 10 on Saturday morning, but others continue to leave and the last pilgrims arrive on Sunday night. [Then a pause, and the Pope concluded] That's how I discovered Luján; discovered the Virgin.[13]

In 1992, Jorge Bergoglio discovered devotion to the Virgin of Luján and made it a part of his life.

---

13 AWI MELLO, *Ella es mi mamá*, p. 70.

Pilgrimages to shrines are a *rich and mobile* image of the faith life of the pilgrim people of God through history toward the fullness of the kingdom of God. Each year, almost 80% of Latin American Catholics go on pilgrimage to some Marian shrine. Aparecida teaches:

> We highlight pilgrimages where the People of God can be recognised in their journey. There the believer celebrates the joy of feeling surrounded by myriad brothers and sisters, journeying together toward God who awaits them. Christ himself becomes pilgrim, and walks arisen among the poor. The decision to set out toward the shrine is already a confession of faith, walking is a time song of hope, and arrival is the encounter of love (*DA* 259).

These words appear to be an echo of a text of Bergoglio's which he published in 2004, in a book prepared for the thirtieth anniversary of the youth pilgrimage to Luján. In his reflection, entitled *On Pilgrimage to Luján: Walk, Visit, Encounter, Return,* he explored the pilgrimage from a phenomenological and theological perspective, and saw the pilgrims' attitudes as an inculturated Marian Catechism.[14]

---

14   Cf. JM Bergoglio, 'Peregrinar a Luján: Camino, Visita, Encuentro, Regreso', in: CM GALLI – G DOTRO – M MITCHELL, *Seguimos caminando. La peregrinación juvenil a Luján*, Buenos Aires, Agape, 2004, 27–32; on the hermeneutic of pilgrimage, cf. CM GALLI, 'Imagen plástica y móvil del Pueblo de Dios peregrino in la Argentina. Una interpretación teológico-pastoral de la peregrinación juvenil a Luján', in: *Seguimos caminando*, pp. 312–389.

The encounter at the shrine is expressed in the pilgrims' gaze as they look lovingly at the image of the Virgin. Bergoglio was always impressed by the children looking at their Mother and Mary looking at the pilgrims. In 1999, during the homily for the 25th Youth Pilgrimage to Luján, he highlighted the need for pilgrims to receive the Virgin's gentle gaze. Its title was 'The Virgin's gaze is a gift' and repeated the following phrase as a litany after each paragraph: 'Mother, lavish your gaze on us.'

> Today, after a long walk, we have arrived at this place of rest – because the Virgin's gaze is a place of rest – to talk to her about our concerns. We need her tender gaze, the motherly gaze which unlocks our soul. Her gaze is full of compassion and concern. And therefore, today we say to her: Mother, lavish your gaze on us. Because the Virgin's gaze is a gift it cannot be bought. It is her gift. It is the gift of the Father's and of Jesus on the Cross. Mother, lavish your gaze on us.[15]

The beautiful section of the Aparecida Document on popular spirituality highlights the importance of this exchange of gazes between the Mother of God and her pilgrim children:

> The pilgrim's gaze rests on an image that symbolises God's affection and closeness. Love pauses, contemplates mystery, and enjoys it in

---

15 BERGOGLIO – PAPA FRANCESCO, *Nei tuoi occhi è la mia parola*, p. 39.

> silence. It is also moved, pouring out the full load of its pain and its dreams. The confident prayer, flowing sincerely, is the best expression of a heart that has relinquished self-sufficiency, recognizing that alone it can do nothing. A living spiritual experience is compressed into a brief moment (*DA* 259).

The gaze condenses a profound spiritual experience. It is about seeing and being seen, touching and being touched, embracing and being embraced by the Lord and the Virgin. In his indulgence, manifested in the Incarnation of the Word, God wants us to experience his love, and we love him in a way that befits human nature. The logic of the gaze and contact inspires the Pope's pastoral relationship with others. We all need to be seen, heard, and embraced with love.

> There is a need for contact. It is necessary to touch the people, caress them. Touch is the most religious of the five senses. It does good to stretch out our hand to children, the sick, shake hands, caress… Look silently into their eyes. This is also contact.[16]

In 2016, in his address to the Bishops as part of his pastoral visit to Mexico, Francis referred to the exchange of gazes between the people and *La Morenita*.

He confessed he had reflected much on the mystery of this gaze and that he wanted to gaze on her and be reached by the tenderness of her eyes:

---

16 SPADARO, *Le orme di un pastore*, XVII.

I know that by looking at the Virgin's eyes, I can see the gaze of your people who have learned to show themselves in Her. I know that no other voice can speak as profoundly of the Mexican heart as the Virgin speaks to me of it. She cares for their greatest desires, their profoundest hopes. She gathers up their joys and tears. She understands their many languages and replies to them with the tenderness of a Mother because they are her children... As St Juan Diego did, and successive generations of the sons and daughters of the Guadalupan have done, the *Pope too, from this time on, cultivated the desire to look on her. Even more so did I want to be reached by her maternal gaze.* I have reflected much on this mystery of her gaze and I ask them what they receive or what springs from my heart as a Pastor at this moment. Above all the 'Brown Virgin' teaches us that the only force capable of winning over people's hearts is God's tenderness. That which enchants and attracts, which vanquishes and overcomes, which opens and unchains, is not the strength of instruments or the toughness of the law, but the omnipotent weakness of divine love which is the irresistible strength of his gentleness and the irreversible promise of his mercy.[17]

---

17   Francisco, 'Con coraje profético. Discurso a los Obispos de México', *L'Osservatore romano*, 28/2/2016, p. 3.

In 2013, Francis offered an interpretation of the Marian event at Aparecida to the Bishops of Brazil by seeing the Black Virgin as a loving expression of God's humility:

> At Aparecida, God offered his own Mother to Brazil. But at Aparecida God also gave us a lesson about himself, his way of being and behaving. It was a lesson of the humility which is an essential feature fo God's and is part of God's DNA. At Aparecida there is something perennial to learn about God and the Church; a teaching that neither the Church in Brazil nor Brazil itself must not forget.[18]

Beginning with the history of Our Lady of Aparecida, he drew out lessons for the Church's mission. The Church's strength is hidden in the deep waters of God where she must cast her nets. Not only the fishermen, but the image of the Virgin is a sign. Her head and body, which had been separated, were found in the river and put back together. Besides, amid the slavery experienced in colonial Brazil, the Virgin showed herself first divided, then later put back together, in the fishermen's hands. God's beauty reflected in his Mother's face emerges from the darkness of the river. The Black Virgin appeared at a crossroads between Rio de Janeiro, Sao Paulo and Minas Gerais. Francis observed that God appears at the crossroads and the Church must be a sacrament of reconciliation. This Marian outlook of Pope

---

18 Cf. FRANCISCO, 'Encuentro con el Episcopado Brasileño', in: *La revolución de la ternura. XXVIII Jornada Mundial de la Juventud Río 2013*, Buenos Aires, PPC Cono Sur, 2013, p. 41.

Francis, rooted in our popular piety, is another sign that he eloquently embodies 'the Latin American and Caribbean face of our Church' (*DA* 100).

4. Mary in Aparecida and Aparecida in Francis

The Fifth Conference at Aparecida is a real milestone on the synodal and collegial journey of the Latin American and Caribbean Church. After the Council, the Second Conference was held at Medellín, opened by Paul VI. At that small Latin American Council, our Church broke history in a new way. It received Vatican II, called for the renewal of ecclesial life, thought about transformation of the continent, made an option for the peoples, expressed solidarity with the poor, and encouraged a comprehensive liberation. Between Medellín and Puebla, our historical self-awareness was strengthened.

Paul VI's *Evangelii Nuntandi* made a great impact on the Latin American Church and especially on the magisterium, theology and pastoral ministry in Argentina.[19] The influence it had on Bergoglio attests to this Argentinian reception. At the end of the eighties, he and I were teaching Fundamental Pastoral Theology at the two Theological Faculties in the country on the basis of this Exhortation. It was the basis for the official announcement of the Puebla Conference, the only reception of the text at regional level. Puebla's theme was *evangelization in the present and future of Latin*

---

19   Cf. A Grande, *Aportes argentinos a la teología pastoral y a la nueva evangelización*, Buenos Aires, Ágape, 2011, pp. 67–137 and pp. 917–954.

America. The *Puebla Document* considered the Church as the communion of God's people and family. It included culture in the broader sense and looked at religion as its vital root. It sought a new, vital synthesis between the Catholic Faith and modern culture. It valued popular piety as an actively evangelizing force. It contemplated our originality in the face of the Virgin of Guadalupe.

In the eighties, Puebla became a summary of Pastoral Ministry. Professor Jorge Bergoglio had this document read and studied, and also wrote about its ecclesiology and pastoral theology. Puebla recreated the great teaching of Paul VI on relationships between evangelization (*EN* 17–24), culture (*EN* 48, 60–65) and liberation (*EN* 29–39). The chapter on the evangelization of culture (*DP* 385–443) is a key point because it contains 'the pastoral option of the Latin American Church: evangelization of its own culture in the present and toward the future' (*DP* 394). In this context, popular piety (*DP* 396) and the preferential option for the poor (*DP* 1134) are located, highlighting the evangelizing potential of the baptized and humble people (*DP* 450, 1147). The preferential option for the poor, countering unjust poverty and for social justice, arises from God's freely given love. The chapter on *evangelization, liberation and human promotion* (*DP* 470–506) received the teaching of *Evangelii Nuntiandi* (*DP* 479–490) and drew up integrating formulas like 'liberating evangelization' (*DP* 485, 458) and 'integral liberation' (*DP* 475, 481, 489). The triad of *evangelization, culture and liberation* expresses the major emphases of pastoral theology in Latin America.

The integrating Mariology of Puebla is situated within this framework. Here, the Puebla Document is neatly distinct from Medellín, where there was a certain 'Marian silence' in the absence of mentions of the Virgin in its sixteen documents. Between parentheses, this reflects the 'perplexity' (*MC* 58) of the early post-conciliar period (1964–1974) during which it took time to assimilate the conciliar reorientation of Mariology. Whereas, beginning with Puebla, the Conferences contemplated the face of Our Lady of Guadalupe as 'the great sign of the maternal and merciful face of the closeness of the Father and Christ (*DP* 282) and a 'Great example of perfectly inculturated evangelization' (*SD* 15).

On this synodal and collegial journey of the Latin American Church, we find the Fifth Conference of Bishops being held in the Marian Shrine of *Our Lady of the Immaculate Conception, Aparecida* in Brazil (*DA* 1–3, 547).[20] It was a decisive milestone on our journey, in continuity with earlier Assemblies (*DA* 9, 16). It was a religious, ecclesial and evangelizing event that reflected the primacy of action of the divine, and communion between God and his people. Its theme was *'Disciples and missionaries of Jesus Christ, so that our peoples may have life in him'* with the motto: *I am the Way, the Truth and the Life* (Jn 14:6). I had the grace of participating at Aparecida as a theological expert appointed by Benedict XVI and of working with the Editorial Commission.

---

20   Cf. CM GALLI 'Synodalität in der Kirche Lateinamerikas', *Theologische Quartalscrift* 196/1 (2016) pp. 75–99.

Cardinal Bergoglio presided over the commission which drew up the Document. Then, as Pope, he quoted it twenty times in *Evangelii Guadium*.

Yesterday, Bergoglio contributed to Aparecida; today Aparecida helps Francis. The Pope creatively launches some of its major directions in his pastoral program. With his pontificate, the dynamic of missionary conversion driven from the Latin American periphery, is enriching the entire Church. It is clear that the historical significance of the Conference, which encourages a more missionary Church, grew with Francis.

Two weeks after its conclusion, he wrote a first interpretation of the significance of Aparecida.[21] A little later, in August 2007, along with Cardinal Bergoglio, we presented the document to the press. Knowing the history of Latin American pastoral work, I said that if we look at the immediate future and it is put into action perseveringly, this missionary project will involve a good part of the 21st Century. A decade later, Francis is confirming the validity of Aparecida and conferring strategic importance on it in his missionary program for the future. Yet he does not want to export a Latin American model, but wants each Church to

---

21 Cf. CM GALLI, 'Aparecida, ¿un nuevo Pentecostés en América Latina y el Caribe?', *Criterio* 2328 (2007) pp. 362–371. This article, prior to the final version of the Document, was cited by G GUTIÉRREZ, 'La opción preferencial por el pobre en Aparecida', *pp.* 206 (2007) pp. 6–25; JC SCANNONE, 'Primeros ecos de la Conferencia de Aparecida', *CIAS* 568/9 (2007) pp. 343–363; and P HÜNERMANN, 'Kirchliche Vermessung Lateinamerikas: theologische Reflexionem auf das Dokumente von Aparecida', *Theologische Quartalschrift* 188/1 (2008) pp. 15–30.

take up the mission in an inculturated form in its own time and place (*EG* 27, 30, 117).

In 2013, before the authorities of CELAM gathered in Rio de Janeiro, Francis indicated four original characteristics of this assembly.

a) The work did not begin with an *instrumentum laboris* but brought the contributors of the different Sees together in a summary document and began from the pastors' concerns.

b) It developed in a climate of prayer, together with the Brazilian Catholic people whose hymns and prayers offered 'background music' to the work sessions.

c) With the desire of cooperating to bring about a new Pentecost in the Church, the Assembly did not limit itself to producing a document, but took on the task of leading *an ongoing continental mission*.

d) It was the first Conference held in a Marian shrine beneath the maternal protection of the Black Virgin of Brazil (*DA* 1) where pilgrims 'edified and evangelized us' (*DA* 3).[22] This Basilica became an enormous house of prayer, combining the hubbub of a shrine and the silence of a monastery, and displayed a rich and shifting image of the pilgrim and praying people of God.

---

22 Cf. FRANCISCO, 'Encuentro con el Comité de Coordinación del CELAM', in: *La revolución de la ternura*, p. 59.

Bergoglio led the reflection process and coordinated the drawing up of the concluding document. As well as gaining basic assent, he shaped various aspects of the text. His influence can be seen in: the historical context, the missionary feel, and pastoral spirituality of the *Introduction* (*DA* 1–8) and *Conclusion* (*DA* 547–554); the creative assumption of the see-judge-act reflection method, starting with the theological outlook of the missionary disciple (*DA* 19); the hymn of praise which is grateful for the love of God manifested in the giving up of his Son and the gift of his Spirit (*DA* 20–32); Catholic piety understood as the people's mysticism – a way of encountering Christ (*DA* 258–265); a missionary communication which manifests the joy of evangelizing (*DA* 552–554).

Aparecida calls on the Holy Spirit to arouse a *new Pentecost* in Latin America which encourages an essentially missionary and ongoing evangelization (*DA* 13; 551). A Pentecost calls for 'an attitude of ongoing pastoral conversion' (*DA* 366), for a firm missionary decision (*DA* 367) by all communities and ecclesial structures (*DA* 368).

> All ecclesial structures and all pastoral plans of dioceses, parishes, religious communities, movements, and any church institution must be combined with this firm missionary decision. No community should excuse itself from entering decidedly with all its might into the ongoing processes of missionary renewal and from giving up out dated structures that are no longer helpful for handing on the faith (*DA* 365).

Within this context, we can understand Bergoglio's contribution to Mary's missionary outlook at Aparecida and in *Evangelii Gaudium*. Awi Mello relates that the cardinal put a question to him: *'Shall we make a contribution to this text? It seems to me that the relationship between Mary and the Church could be better expressed.'* They then prepared a contribution to fill a lacuna in the test drawn up in the respective sub-commission. In subsequent drafts, the bishops had suggested corrections (*modi*) using the *placet iuxta modum* procedure, giving their assent and introducing modifications. Awi Mello looks at some of these texts which were not included in the Aparecida Document.

The Aparecida text on *Mary, disciple and missionary* (*DA* 266–272), is in an early section of Chapter 6 entitled *'A Trinitarian Spirituality of Encounter with Jesus Christ.'* Bergoglio made a suggestion for affirming the Virgin's missionary nature starting from the Visitation (Lk 1; 39–58). This text tells us that Mary set out and went with haste to proclaim the gospel. The handmaid of the Lord became a servant to others. The cardinal asked that the following wording be added: *'She was the first to 'go with haste' to bring Jesus and with him grace, the Holy Spirit communicating the joy of salvation. The text is an important biblical foundation for referring to Mary as a missionary, since such foundation appears in no part of the document.'*

The Pope calls the Virgin who hurries to visit and serve Elizabeth *Our Lady of Help*:

> She is the woman of prayer and work in Nazareth
> and she is also Our Lady of Help who sets out

from her town 'with haste' (Lk 1:39) to be of service to others. This interplay of justice and tenderness of contemplation and concern for others is what makes the ecclesial community look to Mary as a model of evangelization (*EG* 288).

In another *modus* that did not succeed, Bergoglio took a line from John Paul II on Mary's 'heaviness of heart' (*RMa* 17). We come across this text in his papal teaching:

> Along this journey of evangelization we will have our moments of aridity, darkness and even fatigue. Mary herself experienced these things during the years of Jesus childhood in Nazareth: 'This is the beginning of the Gospel, the joyful good news. However it is not difficult to see in that beginning a particular heaviness of heart linked with a sort of night of faith – to use the words of Saint John of the Cross – a kinds of 'veil' through which one has to draw near to the Invisible One and to live in intimacy with the mystery. And this is the way that Mary, for many years, lived in intimacy with the mystery of her Son, and went forward in her pilgrimage of faith' (*RMa* 177) (*EG* 287).

Mary's pilgrimage of faith leads to her loving communion with Jesus, her Son and Lord.

Chapter 3
JESUS CHRIST AND MARY

1. *The novelty and joy of Jesus Christ*

Jesus Christ is the *Gospel of God* (Mk 1:1; Rom 1:3). The Church is called to reveal the novelty of the Gospel *sine glossa*, 'the heart of Christ's message' *EG* 34). The *kerygma* of trinitarian, paschal and salvific love. Francis stresses the absolute newness of Jesus Christ (*EG* 11) the New Man (Col 3: 11) who makes all things new (Rev 21: 5). 'He is forever young and a constant source of newness' (*EG* 11).

> The real newness is the newness which God himself mysteriously brings about and inspires, provokes, guides and accompanies in the thousand ways. The life of the Church should always reveal clearly that God takes the initiative, that 'he has loved us first' (1 Jn 4: 19) and that he alone 'gives the growth' (1 Cor 3:7)' (*EG* 12).

In a recent interview, Pope Benedict XVI recognized the new climate of joy, freshness and renewal Pope Francis has brought to the Church. When asked if he was happy with the way Pope Francis was pursuing his pontificate, he replied: 'Yes. A new freshness is being breathed into the Church, a new joy, a new charism which reaches out to people. All this is something beautiful.'[1]

The Church is called to intensify a kerygmatic evangelization. The kerygma is the merciful and saving love of the God who is love, through his Son, and in the Spirit. 'The kerygma is Trinitarian. The fire of the Spirit is given in the form of tongues and leads us to believe in Jesus Christ who, by his death and resurrection, reveals and communicates to us the Father's infinite mercy' (*EG* 164). Trinitarian christocentrism follows the teachings of Paul VI (*EN* 26), John Paul II (*DCG* 99–100) and Benedict XVI (*DCE* 1). Francis says: 'Where your synthesis is, there lies your heart' (*EG* 143). The heart of the faith is summarized in two biblical texts. The first, from St John, proclaims: *God is love* (1 Jn 4:8). The second, from St Paul, teaches: the greatest of these is love (1 Cor 13:13).

Francis believes and professes that the Holy Spirit brings about a harmony of differences from the newness of the gospel, the gift of the Holy Spirit brings harmony because He is the bond of love in the Trinity and the connection of trinitarian communion in the Church (*EG* 130–131, 220, 254). The novelty is that 'He builds up the communion and harmony of the people of God. The same spirit is that harmony, just as he is the bond of love between the Father and the Son' (*EG* 117).

---

1 BENEDICTO XVI, Últimas conversaciones (with P. Seewald), Bilbao, Mensajero, 2016, p. 65. This has been published in English as *Benedict XVI Last Testament,* New York, Bloomsbury, 2017.

A key to this pontificate is evangelical and evangelizing joy. *Evangelii Gaudium* expresses the joy of receiving and giving the Good News of Jesus Christ (*EG* 21). In his address to the Jesuit General Congregation, the Pope said: 'In the two Apostolic Exhortations – *Evangelii Gaudium* and *Amoris Laetitia* – and in the Encyclical *Laudato Si'* I wanted to insist on joy.'[2]

The contemporary Church is living through a time of joy alongside the time of mercy. The symbolic beginning of this grace was the proclamation of the opening address of John XXIII at the Council, entitled *Gaudet Mater Ecclesiae*. The Magna Carta of joy and hope is the Pastoral Constitution *Gaudium et Spes* of Vatican Council II in 1965. Its spiritual echo is found in the Exhortation *Gaudete in Domino* by Paul VI in 1975, and in the repeated call to the joy of faith by the popes who followed, up to *Evangelii Gaudium* in 2013.

As Paul VI did (*EN* 74–80), Francis presents an evangelizing spirituality (*EG* 259–283) in order to overcome the temptations faced by pastoral workers (*EG* 79–106). The heart of the new pastoral stage is the joy of evangelizing versus the individualistic sadness which closes hearts and produces Christians 'whose lives seem like Lent without Easter' (*EG* 6).

Since 1975, Bergoglio has repeated Paul VI's call to the delightful joy of evangelizing.[3] Joy was the attitude which

---

2 Cf. Francisco, «Libres y obedientes», *L'Osservatore romano*, 28/10/2016, p. 7.

3 Cf. JM Bergoglio, 'La dulce y confortadora alegría de predicar', in: *El verdadero poder es el servicio*, Buenos Aires,

Pope Montini stressed as the height of the evangelizing spirit:

> Let us preserve the delightful and comforting joy of evangelizing, even when it is in tears that we must sow... May it be the great joy of our consecrated lives... [And may the world] be enabled to receive the Good News not from evangelizers who are dejected, discouraged, impatient or anxious, but from ministers of the Gospel whose lives glow with fervour, who have first received *the joy of Christ* and who are willing to risk their lives so that the Kingdom may be proclaimed and the Church established in the midst of the world (EN 80).

The Editorial Commission at Aparecida wanted to begin and end the document by renewing this call to evangelizing joy. Aparecida insists on the joy of the encounter with Jesus and of communicating his gospel. Missionary disciples have the calling 'to communicate everywhere, in an outpouring of gratitude and joy, the gift of the encounter with Jesus Christ' (*DA* 14). Joy 'is not a feeling of selfish well-being, but a certainty that springs from faith, that soothes the heart and provides the ability to proclaim the good news of God's love (*DA* 29). As an expert at Aparecida, I can testify that Bergoglio wanted to quote the paragraph from *Evangelii Nuntiandi* 80 at the end of the document (*DA* 552). In 2013,

Claretiana, 2013 (2nd.), 302–315; i*n Él sólo la esperanza*, Madrid, BAC, 2013, pp. 77–84.

Bergoglio expressed this mysticism of joy in his intervention at one of the meetings of cardinals prior to the Conclave. The text, made known on 27 March 2013, records that he quoted the phrase 'the delightful and comforting joy of evangelizing' three times. It echoes his Jesuit heart which thanks the Lord for his consolation and takes on the mission of consoling his people.

Jesus Christ is God's joy for all human beings. The Pope encourages the renewal of evangelical and evangelizing joy (*EG* 83) that 'cannot be taken away from us by anyone or anything' (*EG* 84). 'The joy of evangelizing... is a grace which we constantly need to implore' (*EG* 13). Missionary joy is marked by the dynamic of gift: 'The Gospel joy which enlivens the community of disciples is a missionary joy... This joy is a sign that the Gospel has been proclaimed and is bearing fruit. Yet the drive to go forth and give, to go out from ourselves, to keep pressing forward in our sowing of the good seed, remains ever present' (*EG* 21).

2. *The song of the Magnificat: 'My spirit rejoices in God my Saviour'*

The birth of Jesus Christ, the Saviour, the Messiah, the Lord is a message of joy 'Do not be afraid; for see – I am bringing you good news of great joy for all the people' (Lk 2:10). Before, at the Annunciation, the messenger greeted Mary, telling her: 'Hail, full of grace, the Lord is with you' (Lk 1:28). At the Visitation, Mary brings the Saviour who communicates joy (Lk 1:41, 44). Elizabeth congratulates her for having believed that what the Lord had announced would be accomplished (Lk 1:45). That 'blessed are you' anticipates Mary's joy because all generations would call her blessed (Lk 1:48). The *Magnificat*, in the tradition of biblical hymns, is a prayer based on the Word of God.

> She who 'kept all these things, reflecting on them in her heart' (Lk 2: 19; Cf. 2: 51), teaches us the primacy of listening to the Word in the life of the disciple and missionary. The *Magnificat* *'is entirely woven from threads of Holy Scripture, threads drawn from the Word of God. Hear we see how completely at home Mary is with the Word of God; with the ease with which she moves in and out of it. She speaks and thinks with the Word of God; the Word of God becomes her word, and her word issues from the Word of God...'* (*DCE* 41) (*DA* 271).

Bergoglio, who is a contemplative of the Word of God and preacher of the *Spiritual Exercises*, refers to the Magnificat, which is the basis of the memory of mercy and sings of the joy of the love of *Deus semper maior*, who looked upon the lowliness of his servant. In the *Exercises* he preached to the Spanish bishops in 2006, he indicated that the Magnificat is sung in poverty and humiliation and by placing hope in God alone. In this context he comments on a paragraph from the Jesuit Constitution:

> The Society (the Church), which was not established by human means cannot preserve itself nor increase through those means but

> with the omnipotent hand of Christ, God and our Lord. *It is essential to place hope only in Him*, for Him to preserve and carry forward what he designed to begin, for his service and praise, and for the help of souls.

The Son of God became flesh, poor, a slave. Jesus presented himself among human beings as the one who serves. United with her Son who became a servant, Mary too is the servant of the Lord. The great things the Lord did in her result in a shift from humiliation to exultation. The Magnificat sums up the spirituality of the *anawim* and anticipates the paradoxical logic of the Easter cross. Mary's heart shares Christ's sentiments (Phil 2:5). He emptied himself taking the form of a slave and was exalted above every name and so that every tongue should confess (Phil 2:7–11). Mary sings the greatness of God and recognises that she is his handmaid for which all nations will call her blessed (Lk 1:47–49).[4]

Bergoglio's commentary on this Marian hymn shares Mary's outlook. She helps to see, remember and be grateful for the great things of the Lord who looked mercifully on the lowliness of his servant:

> Mary's outlook in the Magnificat can help us to contemplate this ever greater Lord. The dynamic of the *magis* inspires the rhythm of the Magnificat which is the hymn that lowliness

---

4 Cf. L Deiss, *María, hija de Sión*, Bilbao, Cristiandad, 1967, pp. 164–192, esp. pp. 184–192.

> intones to Greatness. This greatness of the Lord contemplated through the pure eyes of Mary purifies our outlook, purifies our memory in two of its movements: 'remembering' and 'desiring'. Our Lady's outlook in remembering is spirited: nothing casts a shadow over or stains the past, the great things the Lord has done. He 'looked with favour on the lowliness of his servant' and this first love is the basis of her whole life. Hence Mary's is a grateful memory.[5]

At the homily for the inaugural Mass of his Petrine ministry, evoking the example and words of Jesus, Francis said that true power is service.[6] In 2015, in his address at fiftieth anniversary of the establishment of the Synod of Bishops, he referred to synodality as a constitutive dimension of the Church. He then proposed a theology of the *Synodal Church* and used the attractive image of an *inverted pyramid* where the top is below the base:

> Jesus established the Church by placing the Apostolic College at the top in which the Apostle Peter is the 'rock' (cf. Mt 16:18) who must 'confirm' his brothers in faith (Lk 22:32). However, within Church, as in an *inverted pyramid*, the top is found below the base. Hence those exercising authority are called

---

5 JM BERGOGLIO, *En Él sólo la Esperanza. Ejercicios Espirituales a los Obispos españoles*, Madrid, BAC, 2013, p. 10.

6 Cf. FRANCISCO, 'Para custodiar y acoger. Homilía en la Misa en el inicio del ministerio como sucesor de Pedro', *L'Osservatore romano*, 22/3/2013, p. 9.

> 'ministers': because according to the original meaning of the word, they are the least of all. Each bishop, in serving the People of God, becomes a *vicarius Christi* (*LG* 27) for that portion of the flock entrusted to him; a vicar of Jesus who bent down at the Last Supper to wash the feet of his disciples (Jn 13:1–5). From a similar perspective, the successor of Peter is a *servus servorum Dei*.[7]

Synodality understands the hierarchical ministry to be the service of love for the people of God (*LG* 18). Jesus' followers, especially the successors of the apostles, share in his service to all (Mk 10:45). Like St Ignatius, Bergoglio loves to call Mary by the titles of 'Our Lady', 'Madonna', 'Notre Dame', names popularised in the West during the Middle Ages and which were very common at the beginning of modernity. The figure of Mary was growing and took on a relative autonomy in relation to the Church, acquiting features of the 'Patroness' who ensures protection (*patrocinium*) for those who call on her. 'Our Lady' welcomes beneath her protective mantle all who recognize her mercy and power, whatever their social background may be, and who trust in her patronage.[8]

In baroque Catholicism, many men and women sought to become slaves of the Slave who was Mary, Our Lady.

---

7 Francisco, 'Discurso en la Conmemoración del 50 Aniversario de la institución del Sínodo de los Obispos' (17/10/2015), *L'Osservatore romano* 23/10/2015, p. 9.

8 De Fiores, *María, síntesis de valores*, p. 214.

Veneration of the Virgin encouraged 'Marian slavery' through voluntary and irrevocable consecration. This spirituality of loving surrender and humble service characterized a Servant of God called *Negro Manuel* in the 17th Century (+1686). He was born in Cape Verde, taken as a slave to America, went with an image of the Virgin to Luján, was witness to its miracle and lived in the region of today's Republic of Argentina. He dedicated himself to her to be her faithful custodian, and defended her cult. This black layman, a poor slave, whose cause of canonization is in process, repeated a phrase which grasps the paradox of his heart and belonging: *soy de la Virgen nomás*, I am the Virgin's alone.[9] In 2010, at the Mass for the Bicentenary of Argentina at the Shrine at Luján, Cardinal Bergoglio spoke about Negro Manuel as a silent observer of history, and an example of the fidelity of the people 'who intuitively sense Mary's presence and hence trusted her.'[10]

3. Mary as believer, disciple and missionary of the gospel

Evangelii Gaudium takes up the teaching of Paul VI on evangelization. Francis names this Pope five times and quotes his documents twenty nine times, fifteen of them from *Evangelii Nuntiandi*. In 2014, at the Rome Assembly, he said that this Exhortation 'is the best pastoral document of the post-conciliar period. Nothing has surpassed it.'[11] In

---

9   Cf. S Gómez Tey, *El Negro Manuel y su vida en la historia de la Virgen de Luján,* Buenos Aires, Agape, 2017.

10   Bergoglio – Papa Francesco, *Nei tuoi occhi é la mia parola,* p. 774.

11   Francisco, 'Con la puerta abierta… una madre tierna y

an interview with the Spanish Daily, *El País* on 22 January 2016, he said that *Evangelii Gaudium* is an updated synthesis of *Evangelii Nuntiandi* and the *Aparecida Document*, the framework for pastoral activity he wants for the Church. This document had far-reaching effects on the Latin American Church, especially on Pastoral Theology in Argentina.[12] Bergoglio is a living witness to this reception in Argentina.

The Pope wanted us to focus on the mission of *proclaiming the gospel*.[13] His pastoral ecclesiology follows that of Paul VI', because the Church exists 'in order to evangelize' (*EN* 14). He proposes 'the missionary transformation of the Church' (*EN* 19–51). 'A Church which goes forth' (*EG* 20–24) focuses on the human being through mission. Through missionary conversion, the Christian, missionary and disciple of Jesus Christ, takes the focus off him or herself to focus on Christ. Christ calls the missionary disciple for follow him as a disciple and sends him or her as a missionary to the fringes of society and existence.

Francis' project is summed up in three motivational lines: 'missionary outreach is paradigmatic for all the Church's activity'; 'I hope that all communities will devote the necessary effort to advancing along the path of a pastoral

acogedora', *L'Osservatore romano*, 20/6/2014, p 3.

12 Cf. CM GALLI, 'Pablo VI y la evangelización de América Latina. Hacia la nueva evangelización', in: ISTITUTO PAOLO VI, *Pablo VI y América Latina*. Brescia, Publications of the Paul VI Institute 24, 2002, pp. 161–197; A GRANDE, *Aportes argentinos a la teología pastoral y a la nueva evangelización*, Buenos Aires, Ágape, 2011, pp. 67–137 and pp. 917–954.

13 Cf. V FERNÁNDEZ; P RODARI, *Il progetto di Francesco*, Bologna, EMI, 2014, pp. 29–41, esp. p. 31.

and missionary conversion which cannot leave things as they presently are'; 'I dream of a "missionary option", that is, a missionary impulse capable of transforming everything' (*EG* 15, 25, 27). In line with Aparecida he formulates a command that sums things up: 'we are always "missionary disciples"' (*EG* 120).

In this context we gain a better perception of the first statement of the Aparecida Document with its Bergoglian flavour, which recognizes that the children gathered at the Shrine are protected beneath Mary's mantle and that as the perfect disciple of Christ, she helps us to be children and disciples of her Son and Master.

> Mary, Mother of Jesus Christ and of his disciples, has been very close to us, has taken us in, cared for us and our labours, sheltering us like Juan Diego and our peoples, in the folds of her mantle, under her motherly protection. We have asked her as Mother, perfect disciple, and pedagogue of evangelization, to teach us to be sons and daughters in her Son and to do what He tells us (Jn 2:5) (*DA* 1).

Mary, the perfect disciple, is also the pedagogue of the gospel and of evangelization.

> The appearance of Our Lady of Guadalupe was a decisive event for the proclamation and recognition of her Son, a lesson and sign of inculturation of the faith, manifestation and renewed missionary impetus for spreading the Gospel (*DA* 4).

The Mariological section of Aparecida looks at Mary as disciple and missionary (*DA* 266–272).[14]

> Today, when the emphasis is being given to discipleship and mission in our Latin American and Caribbean continent, it is she who shines before our eyes and the complete and absolutely faithful image of the following of Christ. This is the hour of the most radical follower of Christ, of her teaching for discipleship and mission (*DA* 270).

The figure of Mary 'offers the perfect model of the disciple of the Lord' (*MC* 37). Aparecida sees her as disciple and formator of disciples, as missionary and formator of missionaries. This view of her as model, mother and educator of missionary disciples made further progress in the *Summary Document*.[15] This evangelical profile tallies with her evangelizing mission in the history of America.

> Mary is the great missionary, continuer of her Son's mission, who forms missionaries. As she

---

14 The most authoritative commentary is by Mariologist F PETRILLO, an expert at Aparecida and member of the subcommission which drew up the document; cf. 'María, madre y formadora de discípulos misioneros en el Documento de Aparecida', in: CELAM - SECRETARÍA GENERAL, *Testigos de Aparecida* II, Bogotá, CELAM, 2008, pp. 11–44. Mary's gaze as disciple and missionary was the subject of the *Encuentro continental de pastoral mariana y Congreso teológico pastoral-mariano*, organized by CELAM in 2006. The main papers were delivered by S DE FIORES, F PETRILLO, J ALLIENDE and D FLORES; cf. CELAM – SECRETARÍA GENERAL, *María, Madre de discípulos*, Bogotá, CELAM, 2007, pp. 9–309.

15 Cf. CELAM, *Síntesis de los aportes recibidos para la Quinta Conferencia*, Bogotá, CELAM, 2007, nos 186–192.

> gave birth to the Saviour of the world, she brought the Gospel to our Americas. In the Guadalupe event together with the humble Juan Diego, she presided over Pentecost, which opened us to the gifts of the Spirit. Since then, countless communities have found in her the closest inspiration for learning how to be disciples and missionaries of Jesus (*DA* 269).

On the third centenary of the appearance of the Black Virgin and the tenth anniversary of the Fifth Conference, the Pope referred to the Mystery of Aparecida as the school of missionary discipleship.[16]

Above all else, Mary is a *believer* who realizes and reflects the most radical demands of faith of the disciple and missionary. With the magisterium of *Lumen Gentium* and *Redemptoris Mater*, and contemporary Mariology, Aparecida looks at Mary as member, model, mother and teacher of believers.

> The greatest realization of Christian existence as Trinitarian, living as 'children in the Son' is given us by the Virgin Mary, who by her faith (cf. Lk 1; 45) and obedience to God's will (cf. Lk 1:38) and by her constant meditation on the Word and on the actions of Jesus (cf. Lk 2: 19, 51), is the Lord's most perfect disciple (*LG* 53). As the Father's inter locator in his project of sending

---

16 Francisco, 'Carta a la XXXVI Asamblea General del Consejo Episcopal Latinoamericano', *L'Osservatore romano* (Argentinian edition), 20/5/2017, p. 3.

his Word to the world for human salvation, Mary, by her faith, becomes the first member of the community of believers in Christ, and also collaborates in the spiritual rebirth of the disciples. Her figure emerges from the Gospel as a free and strong woman, consciously directed toward true following of Christ. She has fully experienced the entire pilgrimage of faith as mother of Christ and then of the disciples, and yet has not been saved from incomprehension and continually having to seek the Father's project. Thus she came to stand at the foot of the cross in deep communion, so as to then fully enter into the mystery of the covenant (*DA* 266).

For John Paul II, Mary 'is in contact with the truth about her Son only in faith and through faith!' (*RMa* 17) and hence faith 'preserved her union with her Son even to the Cross' (*RMa* 18). Her believing outlook allowed her to enter and share in the redeeming mystery of Jesus and converts her into a special 'witness' of his person and his work. Hence the Church, as a believing community, 'from the very first moment, "looked at" Mary through Jesus, just as she "looked at" Jesus through Mary' (*RMa* 26).

In the section *Blessed is she who believed* of his first Encyclical *Lumen Fidei*, Francis contemplates Mary (*LF* 58–60). In the fullness of time, the Word of God was addressed to Mary. She welcomed it in her heart so that it might take flesh in her and be born as light for all people. Joy is the most evident sign of faith. In her life, Mary carried out the pilgrimage of faith, following her Son. In her, the journey of faith of the Old Testament was taken up in her following of Jesus. She allowed herself to be transformed by him, and took on the outlook of the incarnate Son of God. Through her blessed faith Mary is intimately associated with her Son, who is the only Son of the Father. On the other hand, Mary's true motherhood ensured that the Son of God had a true human history, true flesh, in which he would die on the cross and rise from the dead.

> Mary will accompany Jesus to the cross (cf. *Jn* 19:25), whence her motherhood will extend to each of his disciples (cf. *Jn* 19:26–27). She will also be present in the upper room after Jesus resurrection and ascension, joining the apostles in imploring the gift of the Spirit (cf. *Acts* 1:14). The movement of love between Father, Son and Spirit runs through our history, and Christ draws us to himself in order to save us (cf. *Jn* 12:32). At the centre of our faith is the confession of Jesus, the Son of God, born of a woman, who brings us, through the gift of the Holy Spirit, to adoption as sons and daughters (cf. *Gal* 4:4) (*LF* 59).

'Mary treasured all these words and pondered them in her heart' (Lk 2:19). Her faith displayed a simple and fundamental truth: 'the Mother of God is pure creature' as St Thomas Aquinas said when clarifying the kind of veneration due the Virgin (*ST* III, 25, 5, sc). In the 20th Century, Romano Guardini was one of the first to carry out an existential understanding of Mary. In his youthful work (*Polar Opposition*), he explored concrete humanity and analyzed the dialectical rhythm running through life.[17] The German-Italian thinker called the bond existing between two realities 'opposition' – they mutually attract and repel each other, yet one cannot be absorbed by the other. In this theory of polar opposition the human being is made up of pairs which are in principle opposites and correlation, such as similarity/distinctiveness, newness/continuity, unity/plurality, and many others. This cosmic view helped him to think of questions like the relationship between Christianity and the world, seeking a higher unity which keeps the polar tensions.

Guardini did not produce a Mariology, but he established fundamental criteria in his brief work *The Mother of the Lord*. Distancing himself from both overstatement and underestimation, he wanted to stress that she is a human being, not a god-like mother or superhuman. He emphasized the fact that Mary did not come to fullness *a priori*, but she grew in faith, especially in her relationship with her Son. The peculiarity of the Marian approach is 'faith which perseveres with the incomprehensible, looking at what God brings to light.'[18] Tacitly, he applied his theory of opposites to closeness and distance: 'Thus, in her relationship with her

---

17 R Guardini, *Der Gegensatz. Versuche zu einer Philosophie des LebendigKonkreten* (1925), Mainz, Grünewald, 1985, 169–174; cf. D. Fares, 'Prefazione', in: *L'opposizione polare*, Milan, La Civiltá Cattolica, 2014, V–XI.

18 R Guardini, *La Madre del Señor*, Madrid, Guadarrama, 1965, p. 71.

Son, while in closest confidence, there had to be a distance, a certain lack of understanding which also shows up in some Gospel accounts.'[19]

Pope Francis thinks of ways of overcoming opposites, while maintaining differences and taking on tensions. He brings Guardini's theory into reality by regarding the higher unity which integrates opposites in tension. Hence he proclaims that 'unity is greater than conflict' (*EG* 228) and 'the whole is greater than the part' (*EG* 235). The unity of the Spirit harmonizes all diversity, including the dialectical dispersion which affects personal interiority and social coexistence. Guardini's philosophy helps the Pope discern the fullness of human experience in each era (*EG* 224, note 182) and the paradigm of technocratic globalized power (*LS* 101–136).[20] Although I do not know of a text in which he refers to Guardini's work on Mary, in another study he analyzed and employed polar opposites for thinking with and leading the Church.[21] In an interview in 2016 he explained this mindset:

> Opposites opens a path, a way to go. Speaking more generally, I have to say that I love opposites. Romano Guardini helped me with his book *Polar Opposition*, which is important

---

19   R Guardini, *La Madre del Señor*, p. 64.

20   Cf. R Guardini, *El fin de los tiempos modernos*, Buenos Aires, Sur, 1973; *El poder*, Madrid, Guadarrama, 1963.

21   Cf. CM Galli, 'La riforma della Chiesa secondo Francesco. L'ecclesiologia del popolo di Dio', in: A Spadaro; CM Galli; (ed.), *La riforma e le riforme nella Chiesa*, Brescia, Queriniana, 2016, pp. 27–55.

for me. He spoke of a polar opposition in which two opposites do not cancel out one another. It doesn't happen that one pole destroys the other. There is neither contradiction nor identity. For him, opposition is resolved on a higher plane. Bipolar tension continues in that solution. The tension remains, is not abolished. Limits are overcome, not denied. Opposites help. Human life is structured by opposites. And that is what also happens in the Church.[22]

4. *The revolution of tenderness: 'Through the loving mercy of our God'*

The God who is 'rich in mercy' (Ex 34:6; Eph 2:4) is reflected in the fact of Christ. God always surprises us with the free initiative of his love. Since his youth Bergoglio has experienced the merciful gaze of God who loves and forgives. Hence, he chose the words of St Bede the Venerable for his episcopal motto: *Miserando atque eligendo*. Now as successor of the Apostle Peter, he invites the whole Church to trust in the infinite mercy of God.[23] '(The Church) has an endless desire to show mercy, the fruit of its own experience of the power of the Father's infinite mercy' (*EG* 24).

Francis proclaims that *the revolution of God's tenderness* began with the Incarnation of the Word. This expression has Trinitarian, Christological and Marian foundations. In the

---

22 SPADARO, *Le orme di un pastore*, XIX.
23 Cf. CM GALLI, 'El amor y la alegría en *Evangelii gaudium*', in: SOCIEDAD ARGENTINA DE TEOLOGÍA, *La caridad y la alegría: paradigmas del Evangelio*, Buenos Aires, Agape, 2015, pp. 65–103.

eighties, Father Jorge – as he liked to be called – thought of this expression while contemplating the sculpture known as the *Pietà*. He recalled then that in the 15th Century, the *Pietà* depicted the figure of Mary with many children and in the 16th Century began to be represented as the compassionate Mother with her dead Son across her knees, but with a serene look on her face because of the hope of the resurrection. 'The *Pietà* is a skilful expression of the revolution of tenderness with which God wanted to save humankind.'[24]

Later, as Archbishop of Buenos Aires, in his televised Christmas messages Bergoglio contemplated the image of the Child Jesus and said that *God is tenderness*.

Like John XXIII, Francis symbolizes 'the Church of charity,'[25] which becomes gentleness in the caress, the embrace and the kiss. The current Successor of Peter proclaims the relevance of the *time of God's mercy*, the God who comes close to us to touch and heal the different wounds of humanity's suffering flesh (*EG* 3, 44). *The good Pope* – and Francis – responds to the voice of the Lord who says: 'I was in prison and you visited me' (Mt 25:36). At Christmas 1958, John XXIII visited the *Regina Coeli* prison; on Holy Thursday, Francis washed the feet of minors in prison. On 11 October 1962, at the opening of the Council, John XXIII invited the Church to use the medicine of mercy and to let go of the rod of severity; at the *Angelus* on 17 March

---

24 Cf. JM BERGOGLIO, *Reflexiones espirituales sobre la vida apostólica* (1987), Bilbao, Mensajero, 2013, p. 245.

25 Cf. G LAFONT, *L'Église en travail de réforme. Imaginer l'Église catholique* II, Paris, Cerf, 2011, 145–168.

2013, Francis said that God is mercy and never tires of forgiving, but it is we who tire of asking him for forgiveness. In the radio message he gave on 11 September 1962, John XXIII said that the Church must be among the poor and underprivileged, 'the Church of everyone but especially the Church of the poor.' With journalists on 20 March 2013, Francis shared his desire for 'a poor Church for the poor.'

Along with their values and limitations, Francis shares charisms with his immediate predecessors: the prophetic spirit of John XXIII; the prudent discernment of Paul VI; John Paul 1's fresh smile; the missionary zeal of John Paul II; the serene reflectiveness of Benedict XVI. Each in his time reflected, in his own features, the tender humanity of our God. Thus, gentle goodness in Roncalli; patient warmth in Montini – Pope *Megalócardos*, as Patriarch Athenagoras called him in 1965; spirituality and liturgy of God 'rich in mercy' – *Dives in Misericordia* – in Wojtyla; primacy of love in Ratzinger, because *Deus Caritas est*, God is love.

Mercy is the main hermeneutic of Francis' pontificate. In the Bull *Misericordiae Vultus,* he says it is the main beam supporting the life and mission of the Church.[26] On 8 December 2015, he opened the Door of the Jubilee of Mercy on the 50th Anniversary of Vatican II. He called the Council the 'great door' which the Church opened to encounter the people of our time and bring them the joy of the gospel and mercy of God. He said on that day: 'As we pass through the

---

26 W KASPER, *La misericordia*, Santander, Sal Terrae, 2012; *Testimone della misericordia*, Milan, Garzanti, 2015.

Holy Door today may we commit ourselves to making the mercy of the Good Samaritan our own.'[27]

Francis preaches the mercy of God who loves and forgives. He reminds us that Paul VI explained in notes for his last will and testament – known as 'Meditation before death' – that his spiritual life could be summed up in a sentence from St Augustine: 'Misery and mercy; my misery and God's mercy.' In documentation for his process for beatification it reads that one of Paul VI's secretaries said, commenting on this, that he confessed it was a great mystery that as wretched as one might be, one could still live in the presence of God's mercy.[28] In the letter *Misericordia et Misera* Francis presents this perspective and in this context he established the *World Day of the Poor* to 'renew the face of the Church in its perennial action of pastoral conversion, in order to be a witness to mercy.'

The sum of the Christian religion consists in mercy expressed as exterior works (*ST* II–I, 30, *ad 2um*). One source of Francis' theology of mercy is St Thomas Aquinas' *Summa Theologiae* (*EG* 37).[29] This Thomist inspiration is a feature of Argentinian theology which seeks to connect the classic tradition with contemporary reflection. Inspired by Jesus'

---

27 Cf. FRANCISCO, 'Como el buen samaritano', *L'Osservatore romano*, 11/12/2015, p. 7.

28 Cf. FRANCISCO, *El nombre de Dios es misericordia*, (ed. A. Tornielli), Barcelona, Planeta, 2016, pp. 27, 55.

29 In the Exhortation *Evangelii Gaudium* the Summa Theologicae is cited seventeen times: there are 3 mentions in the text (EG 37, 43, 171) and 14 quotes in the notes (35, 40, 44, 47, 48, 93, 105, 117, 133, 166, 191).

words on the final judgement (Mt 25: 31–46), the Christian religion encourages a culture of mercy. This is the historical form of love because we suffer so much misery in our history. The cross reveals that the love of God is stronger than sin, death, evil. Jesus soothes the wounds of our humanity and calls on us to touch the suffering flesh of others. The Pope 'wants us to touch human misery, to touch the suffering flesh of others' (*EG* 270).

Francis integrates all truth and virtue in a harmonious order focused on the *Gospel of charity* (*EG* 34–40). 'In this basic core, what shines forth is the beauty of the saving love of God made manifest in Jesus Christ who died and rose from the dead' (*EG* 36). The Kerygma proclaims this gospel core from which each component of life finds 'a fitting sense of proportion' (*EG* 38). Christian practice, moral teaching and pastoral spirituality emerge from the vitality of the Spirit who guides the Churches (Rev 3:6) and from conversion to the gospel, *sine glossa*, to live our freedom to love (Gal 6:5) with the grace of the spirit. The successor of Peter teaches:

> Saint Thomas Aquinas pointed out that the precepts which Christ and the apostles gave to the people of God 'are very few.' Citing Saint Augustine, he noted that the precepts subsequently enjoined by the Church should be insisted upon with moderation 'so as not to burden the lives of the faithful' and make our religion a form of servitude, whereas 'God's mercy has willed that we should be free.' This warning, issued many centuries ago, is most

timely today. It ought to be one of the criteria taken into account in considering a reform of the Church and her preaching which would enable it to reach everyone (*EG* 43).

The Exhortation *Amoris Laetitia* proclaims the gospel of love and analyzes questions of pastoral ministry to families. The Pope wants to encourage the new generations to experience faithful and fertile love in marriage and the family. In Chapter 8 he teaches: 'The logic of pastoral mercy' (*AL* 307–312) in order to accompany, discern and integrate the weakness of people who experience difficult family situations. It is the 'logic of the Gospel' (*AL* 297), the logic of 'compassion' (*AL* 308), the logic of 'integration' (*AL* 299) which should encourage a serious, integrated and creative pastoral ministry.

Mary is the sublime icon of God's mercy. At the *Angelus* on the solemnity of the Immaculate Conception 2015, at the beginning of the Jubilee of Mercy, Francis said that the Virgin is the dawn of the new creation 'the first to be saved by the infinite mercy of the Father.'[30]

---

30 FRANCESCO, *Maria, aurora del mondo*, p. 13.

Chapter 4
MARY AND THE PEOPLE OF GOD

1. *The pilgrim and evangelizing people of God*

Pope Francis takes up the major directions of systematic and pastoral ecclesiology focused on the biblical and conciliar notion of the 'people of God' (*LG* 9–17). This notion, found 184 times in the Council, was developed in Chapter 2 of the Constitution *Lumen Gentium* entitled: *On the People of God*. Bergoglio always presents the Church as *God's holy and faithful people* (*EG* 95, 130).

> The image of the Church I like is that of the holy, faithful people of God. This is the definition I often use, and then there is that image from the Second Vatican Council's 'Dogmatic Constitution on the Church' (No 12). Belonging to a people has a strong theological value. In the history of salvation God has saved a people. There is no full identity without belonging to a people... The people itself constitutes a subject. And the Church is the people of God on the journey through history, with joys and sorrows.[1]

Francis shares, further explores, and universalizes some ideas that have been called *the Argentinian theology*

---

1 SPADARO, *Intervista a Papa Francisco*, op. cit., p. 459, for English text cf. note 14, p. 26.

*of the people.*² I prefer to call it the *Argentinian theology of the people of God, the people and popular pastoral ministry,* because our tradition has developed two analogous and connected meanings for the concept 'people', one at the ecclesial level and the other at the civic level. They are as strongly dissimilar as they are similar. This line of thought includes an ecclesiology of the people of God, a theology of society, culture and history, and also a pastoral theology which considers the mission of the Church to the people and combines popular piety with the option for the poor.³ Its great exponents were Argentinians Lucio Gera (1924–2012),⁴ and Rafael Tello (1917–2002), today studied in relation to Francis.⁵ Its better known current representative is Juan Carlos Scannone. The great novelty of Francis' pontificate includes the small novelty of a first understanding of this incipient theology which includes 'an ecclesiology of

---

2 Cf. JC SCANNONE, *La teología del pueblo*, Santander, Sal Terrae, 2017, pp. 15–93, 181–274.

3 Cf. CM GALLI, 'El 'retorno' del 'Pueblo de Dios'. Un concepto - símbolo de la eclesiología del Concilio a Francisco', in: V. R. AZCUY; J. C. CAAMAÑO; C. M. GALLI, *La Eclesiología del Concilio Vaticano II. Memoria, Reforma y Profecía*, Buenos Aires, Agape – Facultad de Teología, 2015, pp. 405–471.

4 Cf. CM GALLI, 'Lucio Gera, buen pastor y maestro de teología', in: L. GERA, *Meditaciones sacerdotales*, V. AZCUY; J. CAAMAÑO; C. M. GALLI (eds.), Agape, Buenos Aires, 2015, pp. 15–43.

5 Cf. A FIGUEROA DECK, *Francis, Bishop of Rome*, New York, Paulist Press, 2016, 36–59; R LUCIANI, *El Papa Francisco y la teología del pueblo*, Madrid, PPC, 2016, 21–88; E CUDA, *Para leer a Francisco, Teología, ética y política*, Buenos Aires, Manantial, 2016, pp. 67–158.

the people of God in particular.'⁶ The theology of the people of God reappears with the Argentinian Pope, recovering the central place given it by Vatican II and which lost focus since 1985 in other documents of the papal magisterium.

The Theology Faculty in Buenos Aires celebrated its centenary in 2015.⁷ In 1965, it was a pioneer in commentary on *Lumen Gentium*.⁸ Already then it showed the unity of its first two chapters, beginning with the categories of *Mystery and People*. The 'mystery of the Holy Church' (*LG* 5) is realized in history in the shape of 'a people' (*LG* 9). This pair is the systematic architecture of *Lumen Gentium*. In a paper he delivered in 1989 to the Theological and Pastoral Team of CELAM at Belo Horizonte, I illustrated the original Argentinian reception of the concept of the people of God.⁹ Besides, our theology understood the *world* – which *Gaudium et Spes* speaks of – through the realities and categories of *people* and *culture*. For this, it thought of the people as an historical, cultural and political community in constant gestation. It understood the relationship between the Church and the world as the incarnated or inculturated

6   Cf. W KASPER, *Papa Francesco. La rivoluzione della tenerezza e dell'amore*, Brescia, Queriniana, 2015, 57–69.

7   Cf. CM GALLI, 'La recepción del Concilio Vaticano II en nuestra incipiente tradición teológica argentina (1962–2005)', in: J CAAMAÑO; G. DURÁN; F ORTEGA; F TAVELLI, *100 años de la Facultad de Teología. Memoria, presente, futuro,* Buenos Aires, Fundación Teología y Cultura - Agape, 2015, 2015, pp. 341–387.

8   Cf. R FERRARA; L GERA ET ALII, '*Lumen gentium.* Comentario de la Constitución conciliar sobre la Iglesia', *Teología* 7 (1965) 127–153 y 8 (1966) 3–105.

9   Cf. CM GALLI, 'La Iglesia como Pueblo de Dios', in: CELAM, *Eclesiología.* Bogotá, CELAM 117, 1990, pp. 91–152.

presence of the faith of the people of God in the cultures of the peoples.

Let us try to develop *an integrating ecclesiology* along these lines. The Church is the communion of the people of God in history, or the mystery of the pilgrim people of God in communion. The notions of communion or sacrament are employed *in a predicative or attributive sense*. The Church is a communion but we do not say that communion is the Church, because that is an analogous concept predicated of distinct subjects such as the Trinity, Eucharist, the Church, the family. But the title 'people of God' indicates the subject and is a subjective concept. The people of God is a 'we', the social and historical subject of the mystery and, as such, 'remains irreplaceable.'[10]

These meanings of the term 'people' are in the Exhortation *Evangelii Gaudium*. Chapter 3 speaks of the Church as the pilgrim people of God in history and incarnated in cultures (*EG* 115). Chapter 4 teaches that to build a people requires cultivating the sense of belonging by a 'multifaceted culture of encounter' (*EG* 220). In the interview he gave to introduce the Italian edition of his addresses and homilies as Archbishop of Buenos Aires (1998–2013), the Pope returned to pointing out both distinct and complementary meanings.[11]

---

10 Cf. H Pottmeyer, 'Dal sinodo del 1985 al grande Giubileo dell'anno 2000', in: R Fisichella (ed.), *Il Concilio Vaticano II. Recezione e attualità alla luce del Giubileo*, Turin, San Paolo, 2000, pp. 11–25, 22.

11 Cf. Spadaro, *Le orme di un pastore*, XV–XVI.

For Francis, this 'People of God is incarnate in the peoples of the earth, each of which has its own culture' (*EG* 115). The section 'A people of many faces' (*EG* 115–118) develops the image of the face in the ecclesial sense. Quoting John Paul II he states: 'in the diversity of peoples who experience the gift of God, each in accordance with its own culture, the Church expresses her genuine catholicity and shows forth 'the beauty of her varied face" (*EG* 116; NMI 40). This varied face of the people of God expresses the interculturality of current Christianity.

The people of God is the communal subject of the evangelizing mission of the peoples of the world. Chapter 3 of *Evangelii Gaudium* carries the title: '*The entire people of God proclaims the Gospel*' (*EG* 111–134). What belongs to the whole people of God belongs to everyone in the people of God. It is the great communal evangelizing subject (*EG* 111, 120) and, within its communion, each Christian is called to be an active player in the evangelizing mission (*EG* 121). This papal document is not aimed only at organized pastoral workers but at the simple Christian faithful: 'all of us are called to mature in our work as evangelizers' (*EG* 121) and 'we are always 'missionary disciples" (*EG* 120).

2. *Mary's motherhood and the maternal dimension of the Church*

When preaching the *Spiritual Exercises*, Jorge Bergoglio said that from the very first Rule on 'thinking with the Church' St Ignatius of Loyola employed three images for speaking about her: the Church militant, the Lord's Bride, and Holy Mother (*SE* 352–353).[12] Indeed, Ignatius speaks of 'our Holy Mother the Hierarchical Church' (*SE* 353, 363). In the *Exercises* he preached to the Spanish bishops in 2006, Bergoglio spoke about the profound bonds existing between Mary and the Church:

> Jesus *founds* the Church and we are *founded* in the Church. The mystery of the Church is very much connected with the mystery of Mary, the Mother of God and Mother of the Church. Mary begets and cares for us. The Church too. Mary makes us grow. The Church too. At the hour of our death the priest sends us off in the name of the Church to leave us in Mary's embrace: 'A woman clothed with the sun, with the moon under her feet and on her head a crown of twelve stars (Rev 12:1). This is the Church and this is the Virgin who venerates our faithful people. Therefore, in referring to the Church we need to feel the same devotion as for the Virgin.[13]

Having commented on the expression *Holy Mother Hierarchical Church*, Bergoglio adds that the Church's maternity ties three concepts together: holiness, fecundity and discipline. Holiness of the Church because we were begotten by God in the holy body of the Church. She is reflected in the clear, pure face of Mary Immaculate. The fecundity of the Church begets children with the strength of faith, Mary's faith which gave birth to the Word of life. Motherhood comes about through the paradoxical fecundity of the gospel. Discipline, or disciplined love is part of the

---

12 Cf. BERGOGLIO, *Meditaciones para religiosos*, p. 128.
13 BERGOGLIO, *En Él sólo la Esperanza*, pp. 120–121.

ecclesial body and results in servants of evangelization, which is an 'ecclesial act' (*EN* 60). Discipline is a dimension of holy and fecund love. Membership of the kingdom joins us with Christ's side, asleep on the cross, from whence the Church emerges, his Bride, fertile Mother of the disciplined Body fed by the Eucharist.

> Our love for the Church must lead us to express it before the world for its holiness, warm fecundity and its discipline which is to be completely from Christ and, as the Council says, the *Dei Verbum religiose audiens et fidenter proclamans* (*DV* 1). May Our Lady, the Virgin Mother, obtain for us from the Lord the grace of a holy, fecund and disciplined lover for the Church.[14]

Francis ties the notions of 'People' and 'Mother' to the Latin patristic tradition,[15] and to contemporary ecclesiology.[16] Time and time again he says that the Church is 'woman' and he likes feminine images of the Church: virgin, bride, mother, widow. Above all she is 'a Mother with an open heart' (*EG* 46–49) which recalls Aparecida's

---

14 BERGOGLIO, *En Él sólo la Esperanza*, 128.

15 Cf. Y CONGAR, 'Au lecteur. Préface de Yves Congar', in: K DELAHAYE, *Ecclesia Mater chez les Péres des trois premiers siècles. Pour une renouvellement de la Pastoral d'aujourd'hui*, Paris, Cerf, 1964, pp. 7–32.

16 Cf. H DE LUBAC, 'La maternidad de la Iglesia', in: *Las iglesias particulares en la Iglesia universal*, Salamanca, Sígueme, 1974, pp. 143–231; HU VON BALTHASAR, 'La maternidad envolvente de la Iglesia', in: *El complejo antirromano. Integración del Papado en la Iglesia universal*, Madrid, BAC, 1981, pp. 185–229.

line: 'a mother who reaches out' (*DA* 370). The Church is a Mother with an open heart and a home with open doors so the faithful who live at home may go out to meet all their brothers and sisters (*EG* 46).

> The Church is called to be the house of the Father, with doors always wide open. One concrete sign of such openness is that our Church doors should always be open, so that if someone, moved by the Spirit, comes there looking for God, he or she will not find a closed door (*EG* 47).

Recalling what he told his priests in Buenos Aires, Francis reiterates that he prefers an outgoing Church, on the move and on the street (*EG* 106), even though it may be 'bruised, hurting and dirty,' and not a fearful, quiet and enclosed community (*EG* 49) which will certainly sicken. If the Church gets *out on the street* in the best sense of these words, a wonderful exchange takes place: the pastoral community goes out, other people come in.[17]

Francis stresses the compassionate motherhood of the people of God as a whole, a theme to which he has dedicated a number of his sessions of catechesis.[18] At his meeting with

---

17 Cf. C Bacher Martínez – J Cervantes, 'Callejear en el sentido más amplio… Entrevista al Cardenal Jorge M. Bergoglio sj', in: V Azcuy (ed.), *Ciudad vivida*, Buenos Aires, Guadalupe, 2014, pp. 239–244.

18 Cf. Francisco, 'Cuando la Iglesia nos ha dado a luz', *L'Osservatore romano*, 13/9/2013, p. 12; 'En la universidad de las mamás', *L'Osservatore romano*, 20/9/2013, p. 12.

the Brazilian bishops he spoke of the Church's pastoral maternity:

> Regarding pastoral conversion, I would like to remind you that 'pastoral' is none other than the exercising of the Church's maternity. The Church brings to birth, suckles, brings up, corrects, feeds, gives a hand… it requires a Church capable of rediscovering the maternal feelings of mercy. Without mercy little can be done today to be part of a wounded world which needs understanding, forgiveness and love.[19]

The Church is a Mother because she conceives, accompanies, educates and guides the life of faith of her children and brothers and sisters toward the Father. The people of God has features of woman and Mary, the Woman clothed in the sun represents the people of God. The Word of God refers to the *parallel between people–woman* to Israel. It calls Israel the 'Bride of the LORD,' 'daughter of Sion,' 'Jerusalem a mother.' Jerusalem symbolizes the people of God. She is a mother (Is 51:20; 60:41; 66:10–12) without ceasing to be a virgin (Jer 14:17; Am 5:2; Is 37:2; Lam 2:13). In Israel by virtue of choice and covenant, God is the Father and the people in its City are personifications of the Mother, a figure which in a radical and eminent way realizes the fertile love of God himself.

The New Testament applies these images to the Church as the 'chaste virgin' (2 Cor 11:2), 'joined to the husband'

---

19 FRANCISCO, *Encuentro con el Episcopado Brasileño*, pp. 49–50.

(Eph 5:22–23), and 'fruitful mother' (Gal 4:25–28). The Johannine tradition likens the Church's motherhood and Mary's to the woman who gives birth to the Messiah and the messianic people (Jn 2:1–11, 19:25–27; Rev 12:1–18), antitype of Eve, the woman and mother of the living.

There is a profound correlation between *Church-Mother* and *Church-People*. 'Between the idea of the people of God and the idea of the Church as Mother, there is no adequate distinction,'[20] de Lubac maintained. Von Balthasar said that if the image of the Church as Mother seems strange, it could well be replaced by the better-known people of God.[21] Delahaye, after his study on the motherhood of the people of God in the Fathers of the first centuries, concluded that the pastoral-maternal action by which the life of Christ is begotten in human beings, corresponds to the whole of the ecclesial community.[22] In communicating spiritual life, the Church works as 'a unique subject of action.'[23] The maternal dimension corresponds to the whole people of God inasmuch as it is the community, subject of faith, liturgy, holiness and mission, because 'it is the whole that acts.'[24]

The feminine, maternal and family nature of the people of God is tied to Mary. Faith recognizes a 'mysterious continuity between Marian experience and the maternal experience

---

20 H DE LUBAC, *Paradoja y misterio de la Iglesia*, Salamanca, Sígueme, 1967p. 88.

21 Cf. VON BALTHASAR, *El complejo antirromano*, p. 189.

22 DELAHAYE, *Ecclesia Mater* 204: 'l'action pastorale d'ensemble est avant tout l'affaire de toute l'Église'.

23 CONGAR, *Au lecteur. Préface de Yves Congar*, p. 16.

24 CONGAR, *Au lecteur. Préface de Yves Congar*, p. 12.

of the Church.'²⁵ The correlation between Mary and the Church contemplated from the maternal perspective,²⁶ justifies speaking both of the *maternal dimension*,²⁷ and the *Marian dimension of the Church*.²⁸ In ecclesial motherhood, it is seen that the whole Church is Marian and that Mary is the union of the ecclesial mystery – Mary cares for the brothers and sisters and disciples of her Son (Jn 19:25–27). The Church extends Mary's motherhood and learns spiritual motherhood from her. In the Church, the Mother of God 'stands out in eminent and singular fashion as exemplar both of virgin and mother' (*LG* 63). She is the real symbol and personified representation of the Church as Mother with a 'maternity which embraces both the ecclesiastical maternity and the rest of the people of God.'²⁹ There is a certain 'perichoretic [think of a circle dance or circular movement] identity' between the Virgin and the Church, a loving union which leads to understanding them in their reciprocity, each in and for the other. Mary is Mother, the Church is Mother. Hence, in 1964 Paul VI, considering both poles, declared the formula 'Mary, *Mother* of the Church.'³⁰

Mary's maternity 'is the sacramental presence of God's maternal features' (*DP* 291).

25 De Lubac, *Paradoja y misterio de la Iglesia*, p. 113.
26 Cf. LG 6065; DP 282291; RMa 4244, CEC 963970.
27 H de Lubac, *Meditación sobre la Iglesia*, Pamplona, DDB, 1957, 229269.
28 Cf. HU von Balthasar, *Theodramatik* II/2, Einsiedeln, Johannes, 1978, pp. 260330.
29 von Balthasar, *El complejo antirromano* p. 199.
30 Regarding this formula, cf. De Lubac, *Paradoja y misterio de la Iglesia*, p. 110.

> Mary is truly Mother of the Church. She marks the People of God. Paul VI makes a concise formula of the tradition his own: 'The Church cannot be referred to as such unless it includes Mary' (*MC* 28). It is about a feminine presence which creates the family setting, the desire to welcome, love and respect for life. It is the sacramental presence of the maternal features of God. It is a reality so fundamentally human and holy that it arouses prayers of tenderness, sorrow and hope in believers (*DP* 291).

'At the moment she said 'yes', Mary is Israel in person, the Church in person and as person.'[31] Mariology looks at Mary and the Church from the perspective of the person and woman who is virgin, spouse and mother. This relationship is identity in difference and difference in identity. The key is the paradoxical principle that Mary is an exceptional person and, at the same time, represents the Church in its historical, eschatological totality. The more a person represents a community the more that person is both identified with the reality represented and different in his or her individuality.[32] Being who she is, Mary is a relational person who represents the Church.[33]

---

31 RATZINGER, *Maria – Chiesa nascente*, p. 25.
32 Cf. H MENCKE, *Stellvertretung. Schlüsselbegriff christlichen Lebens und theologische Grundkategorie*, Einsedeln, Johannes, 1997, p. 31.
33 Cf. GRESHAKE, *Maria – Ecclesia*, pp. 433, 440, 442, 456, 458, 460, 463.

3. The feminine correlation between Mary, the Church and the faithful Christian

The core of Francis' Mariology is found in the following paragraph of his agenda-setting Exhortation:

> The close connection between Mary, the Church and each member of the faithful, based on the fact that each in his or her own way brings forth Christ, has been beautifully expressed by Blessed Isaac of Stella; 'In the inspired scriptures, what is said in a universal sense of the virgin mother, the Church, is understood in an individual sense of the Virgin Mary... In a way, every Christian is also believed to be a bride of God's Word, a mother of Christ, his daughter and sister, at once virginal and fruitful... Christ dwelt for nine months in the tabernacle of Mary's womb. He dwells until the end of the ages in the tabernacle of the Church's faith. He will dwell forever in the knowledge and love of each faithful soul' (*EG* 285).

This is one of the Jesuit Pope's favourite Marian texts. It belongs to Blessed Isaac of Stella, the Cistercian abbot at the Monastery of Stella, in France, in the 12th Century. His Marian ecclesiology is taken up by Francis in his teaching. He told Fr Awi Mello: 'It is something I have deep within me, isn't that so?' pointing to his heart. 'Isaac of Stella, from the Monastery at Stella – it is he who made all these reflections.' The Pope has always referred to this text and the analogy it makes between Mary, the Church and the faithful. Here it is good to follow the account of the Brazilian Mariologist.[34]

Bergoglio made a contribution to Aparecida's Mariology on the relationship between Mary and the Church. One day he said to his assistant: 'Please find the exact quote from Isaac of Stella for me, the one that speaks of the relationship between Mary, the Church and the human soul.' Using his text, he presented a suggestion that was incorporated almost literally into No. 268. The original *modus* included Isaac's text which was not added by the Editorial Commission. It said:

'Isaac of Stella states: "*In the divinely inspired Scriptures, what is said in a universal sense of the Virgin Mother, the Church refers in a special sense to the Virgin Mother, Mary.*"'

The proposal continued with a quote from Ratzinger which refers to a text of von Balthasar's: '*In fact the Church is a woman. She is a mother. She is alive. The Marian view of the Church contrasts strongly and decidedly with a merely organizational and bureaucratic concept of Church. We cannot make the Church, but must be the Church. The bond of communion with Mary leads us to be Church.*'

Bergoglio wanted to explain the relationship between Mary and the Church. The Commission took up the core of his proposal and added two sentences to the end of the text to stress the maternal, compared with the functional:

> As in the human family, the Church-family is generated around a Mother, who confers 'soul'

[34] Cf. Awi MELLO, 'Contribuciones mariológicas al documento de Aparecida', in: *Ella es mi mamá*, 193–211.

and tenderness on shared family life (Cf. *DP* 295). Mary Mother of the Church and model and paradigm of humanity, is shaper of communion. One of the fundamental events of the Church is when the 'yes' sprang forth from Mary. She draws multitudes to communion with Jesus and his Church, as we often experience at Marian shrines. Hence, the Church, like Virgin Mary, is mother. This Marian vision of the Church is the best antidote to a merely functional or bureaucratic Church.

Aparecida establishes a likeness between the Church's and Mary's motherhood. With her tenderness she begets communion in the ecclesial family. The only part of the *modus* which did not end up in the document was Isaac's quote. During the conversation with Awi Mello at Santa Marta, the Pope said he had included the text in *Evangelii Gaudium* and commented thus: 'it deals with that analogous parallelism between what is said about Mary that can be said about the Church and the soul – do you agree?'[35]

In order to recognize some of the sources of the Pope's teaching, it helps to recall that von Balthasar developed the *principle of a Marian profile of the Church* which configures its internal communion, just as the *petrine principle or profile indicates its institutional unity*.[36] Both aspects are independent. In Balthasar's theology, Mary and Peter, two central figures,

35 Cf. AWI MELLO, *Ella es mi mamá*, p. 201.
36 Cf. VON BALTHASAR, 'La maternidad envolvente de la Iglesia' in: *El complejo antirromano, pp.* 185–229.

belong to a broader Christological constellation, Peter in the group or college of the Twelve, blends with John, James and Paul in an apostolic quartet.[37] Mary, Mother of Christ, with her maternal *fiat*, participates in the mystery enveloping her Son Jesus. The Marian principle shares and envelops our ecclesial being.

Bergoglio meditated on the work *El complejo antirromano. Interación del Papado en la Iglesia universal* (The anti-Roman Complex. Integration of the Papacy in the universal Church), in which the theologian from Basel developed his Marian view of the Church. Francis re-assessed the feminine, maternal and merciful dimension, typical of Mary, in contrast to a merely organizational understanding of the Church. He meditated on and quoted the classic *Meditation on the Church* by H. de Lubac, which opened up a Marian ecclesiology,[38] and explained the teaching of the abbot of Stella.[39]

In his famous *Sermon 51*, or first sermon for the feast of the Assumption, the medieval author contemplates these three things together: Mary, the Church and the human soul. He carefully considers the correlation there is between *Mary, Virgin and Mother*, and the *Church, Virgin and Mother*. As Mary is virgin and mother, so is the Church. They conceive by the same Spirit and give birth to the same Son. Mary gives birth to the head and the Church gives birth to

---

37 Cf. VON BALTHASAR, *El complejo antirromano.* pp. 131–146 and pp. 315–340.

38 Cf. DE LUBAC, *Meditación sobre la Iglesia*, 305–369; *Las iglesias particulares en la Iglesia universal*, pp. 143–231.

39 Cf. DE LUBAC, *Meditación sobre la Iglesia*, pp. 337–342.

the members. Mary gives birth without sin and the Church gives birth for the remission of sins. Mary conceives by the Holy Spirit for the birth of Christ at Bethlehem and the Church for the rebirth of Christians in Baptism. Neither Mary nor the Church give birth to Christ totally alone nor independently of one another, but they are and act together. One can say that the Church gives birth to Christians with the collaboration of Mary, the Mother of Jesus. For this tradition, we become mothers and virgins of Christ with Mary, because there is a unity in her between being Virgin and being Mother. Hence not only do we need to imitate her but we also need to be united with her. Mary is the principle of this union because she and the Church have the mission of loving Christ as virgin and giving birth to him as mother. 'Also each faithful soul can be understood rightly in its own peculiar way as spouse of the word of God, as mother, daughter and sister of Christ; as virgin and fruitful.'[40] Isaac says that just as there is 'a Son and many sons,' so also there is 'a Mother and many mothers, a Virgin and many virgins.' We, the faithful, are called in the Church to be mothers of Christ, conceiving him in our hearts, our souls, and also being virgins of Christ, showing him our faithful love and total adherence. For the Fathers and Doctors of the Church *virginity* consists in guarding the integrity of the faith. The Constitution *Lumen Gentium* actualises this teaching and quotes the Cistercian's sermon (*LG* 64 Note 20).

40 Cf. Isaac de la Estrella, 'Sermón 51, o Primer sermón para el día de la Asunción', in: *El misterio de Cristo. Sermones. Padres cistercienses 15*, Azul, Edición del Monasterio Trapense de Azul, 1992, pp. 308–316, 310.

This analogy allows us to apply the same characteristics to Mary, the entire Church and to each faithful soul, something Pope Francis very much likes. Isaac of Stella considers that the texts of the Scriptures which refer to Mary can be applied to the Church and vice versa: 'When it speaks of one or the other in a text, its content is applied almost without distinction to the one or the other.' The paragraph of his sermon most commented on states that what the Wisdom of God says, is said of the Church in a *universal sense* (*universalis, generalis*), of the Virgin Mary in a *special sense* (*specialis*) and of the believing soul in a *particular sense* (*particularis*). What is said of Mary especially (holiness, virginity, maternity etc) can be said of the Church in general and of the faithful in particular. For de Lubac, Isaac introduces the novelty of presenting Mary as a *special* figure between the universal and the particular.[41]

This Marian theology distinguishes and combines the universal, the special and the particular. What applies universally to the Church can be applied in a special way to Mary and in a particular way to the soul of the faithful Christian.

Isaac states that Christ wants to repose in, find his tabernacle in the faithful soul in a particular sense, in Mary in a special sense, in the Church in a universal sense. Each is a temple of God in his or her own way. In this symbolic context, Isaac refers, along the lines of some of the holy Fathers, to three births of Christ: the eternal one from the

---

41   Cf. DE LUBAC, *Meditación sobre la Iglesia*, p. 339, which shows the equivalence between the singular and the special in Isaac.

Father, the temporal one from Mary, and the spiritual one from us, by means of Mary and in us, meaning in each of our hearts. There is a perpetuation of the mystery of Christ who is born by the work of the Holy Spirit and of the Virgin Mary, in the Mysteries of the Church-Virgin and our virginal, spousal souls. The life and mystery of Christ is perpetuated in time through Mary, the Church, and each of us.

At the 2005 Synod, the then Archbishop of Buenos Aires appealed to this theology to show the union of Mary with the Eucharist. He mentioned the rule of Tradition according to which, with different nuances, what is said of Mary is said of the entire Church and of the heart of each Christian.

> Our faithful people believes in the Eucharist as the Eucharistic people in Mary. This people links love for the Eucharist with love for the Virgin our Mother, Our Lady. At the school of Mary, the Eucharistic woman, we can re-read contemplatively the passages in which John Paul II sees Our Lady as the Eucharistic woman and looks at her, not alone but 'in the company' of the People of God. Let us follow the rule of tradition whereby, with different nuances, 'what is said of Mary is said of the soul of each Christian and of the entire Church.' Our faithful people has a true 'Eucharistic attitude' of the action of grace and praise. By recalling Mary, our faithful people is grateful for being remembered by her and this is a truly Eucharistic memorial of love.

> In this regard I repeat what John Paul II said in *Ecclesia de Eucharistia* no. 158: 'the Eucharist has been given to us so that our life, like Mary's, may be completely a Magnificat.'[42]

4. *Mary precedes, accompanies and protects the pilgrim people*

Mary is the woman chosen by God to be the Mother of his Son, sent into this world in the fullness of time (Gal 4:4). She had the unique mission of conceiving, educating and accompanying Jesus to the cross.

> From the cross, Jesus Christ entrusts to his disciples, represented by John, the give of Mary's motherhood, which springs directly from the paschal hour of Jesus: 'And from that hour the disciple took her into his home' (Jn 19:27). Persevering along with the apostles awaiting the Spirit (cf. Acts 1:13–14), she aided in the birth of the missionary Church, imprinting on it a Marian seal that deeply marks its identity (*DA* 267).

Vatican Council II presented Mary as the Mother who accompanies the pilgrimage of the people of God in history. 'In the interim, just as the Mother of Jesus… is the image and beginning of the Church… so too does she shine forth (*praelucet*) on earth…as a sign of sure hope and solace to the people of God during its sojourn on earth' (*LG* 68). This teaching is the basis for the most original section of the

---

42 Cf. Awi Mello, *Ella es mi mamá*, p. 68.

Encyclical *Redemptoris Mater* on Mary's accompaniment, which precedes and accompanies the journey in faith and belief of the people of God. From Pentecost she accompanies 'the Church's pilgrimage through the history of individuals and peoples' (*RMa* 26). With her motherly love she succours all those who come to her to seek 'in her faith support for their own.' (*RMa* 27).

The Pope expresses in his own prayer the fact that Mary protects the life and faith of the believing people: 'There are two Marian antiphons that I very much like to say. One is the *Alma Redemptoris* which is sung especially in Advent, but I say it every day in the morning and evening. The other is the *Sub tuum praesidium* which is the first Marian antiphon of the Latin Church. It has to do with Pokrov, Our Lady of Protection, doesn't it? And the Russian monks say it at times of spiritual disruption. The only safe place to be is under the mantle of the Holy Mother of God.'[43]

It is in this context that the Pope recalls the prayer '*We fly to thy patronage, O holy Mother of God.*' It is an anonymous prayer written in Greek and found in an Egyptian papyrus from the 3rd Century, and is the oldest testimony to faith in Mary's power of intercession, invoking her as Mother of God (*Theotókos*). The subject of the antiphon is ourselves, 'we fly to thy patronage... in our necessities,' perhaps it was a Christian community undergoing persecution. The text presents elements of a profound theology at the beginning of Christianity. The titles given Mary are eloquent ones:

---

43 Awi Mello, *Ella es mi mamá*, p. 83.

'holy', indicative of the primitive Church's faith in Mary's holiness; *Theotókos* – 'She who gives birth to God' – a title the Council of Ephesus (431) used in reference to Mary. The word itself does not appear in the prayer and is replaced by the terms *Mother of God and Virgin*. Mary is called '*glorious*' indicating an initial faith in her destiny together with Jesus, and '*blessed*', which evokes Elizabeth's words: 'Blessed are you among women' (Lk 1: 42). The prayer shows that from the first centuries, the faithful people had recourse to Mary's protection because she heard their please and freed them from danger. This prayer is one of Francis' favourites:

> We fly to thy patronage, O holy Mother of God; despise not our petitions in our necessities, but deliver us always from all dangers, O glorious and blessed Virgin.

'These two antiphons say a lot to me,' Francis confesses when speaking of the *Sub tuum praesidium* and the *Alma Redemptoris Mater*. There are four Marian antiphons in the Western Church, written in Latin and prayed at the end of Compline, each in a liturgical period. They are: *Alma Redemptoris, Regina Coeli, Ave Regina Coelorum*, and *Salve Regina*. The *Alma Redemptoris* is prayed in Advent, but Francis says it every morning and evening. He says: 'With regard to the *Alma Redemptoris Mater*, Mary appears there as she who comes to the aid of those who are 'sinking'. She succours this people who wish to rise again, since they have fallen and want to get up.'

> Mother of Christ, hear thou thy people's cry
> Star of the deep and Portal of the sky!
> Mother of Him who thee made from nothing made.
> Sinking we strive and call to thee for aid:
> Oh, by what joy which Gabriel brought to thee,
> Thou Virgin first and last, let us thy mercy see.

The antiphon combines different titles of Mary [a little less obvious in the traditional English translation]: Mother of Christ (Redeemer), fruitful Mother, Gate of Heaven, Star of the sea. This prayer asks her to help the people who fall and wish to get up again: sinking we strive, and call to thee for aid. In July 2013, the Pope went to the island of Lampedusa to pray for victims of a deadly sinking in the Mediterranean. He asked the Virgin to protect migrants and refugees. He addressed her with the ancient title of *Stella Maris: 'Mary, Star of the Sea, more than once we turn to you to find refuge and peace, to implore protection and aid.'*

Mary's mantle is the place to find her protection. Francis associates her material protection with the Ukrainian devotion of *Our Lady of Patronage*, known as *Pokrov* (protective mantle).

> Images of the Virgin have a place of honour in Churches and houses. In them Mary is represented in a number of ways: as the throne of God carrying the Lord and giving him to humanity (*Theotókos*); as the way that leads to Christ and manifests him (*Hodegetria*); as a praying figure in an attitude of intercession and

as a sign of the divine presence on the journey of the faithful unit the day of the Lord (*Deesis*); as the protectress who stretches out her mantle over the peoples (*Pokrov*), or as the merciful Virgin of tenderness (*Eleousa*). She is usually represented with her Son, the child Jesus, in her arms: it is the relationship with the Son which glorifies the Mother (*RMa* 33).

To understand this component of Francis' pastoral and spiritual Mariology, we have to place ourselves in Flores, the suburb of Buenos Aires where the Pope was born and lived. They lived not far from the Basilica of St Joseph of Flores – where Bergoglio confirmed his priestly vocation – and the Church of Our Lady of Patronage, the headquarters of the Ukrainian Eparchy and Eastern Rite Catholic Church which follows the Ukrainian Byzantine Rite. In front of this Cathedral Church is the icon of Our Lady of Patronage. Mary is standing, arms open, and is stretching a white mantle between her hands as a sign of protection. *Pokrov* means 'mantle' or 'veil' but can also be understood as 'protection' or 'intercession'. In Russia and the Ukraine, each 1 October they celebrate the *Feast of the Protective Mantle*, or *Pokrov*. In the Orthodox and Byzantine Catholic Churches it is known as the Feast of the Intercession of the Mother of God.

In Western Catholic art, the icon of Pokrov is associated with the image of Our Lady of Mercy. In the Eastern icon the veil is small and appears to be stretched between Mary's hands or between two angels. In the Western image Mary appears with an open cloak or mantle and people take shelter beneath it. This image became popular in Italy around the 13th and 14th Centuries as the *Madonna della Misericordia*. We will recover this symbolism by focusing our gaze on the Mother of Mercy. In his Marian conversations at the Vatican, Francis said:

> I like the image of Pokrov, meaning Our Blessed Lady of Patronage, where she is stretching out her mantle so the people can take shelter beneath it. It is saying that Mary is the one who protects, takes care of. This devotion of 'She who takes care of you' has developed throughout history.

The Pope expresses his awareness of Mary's motherly care with the life of each and every person. When he sends a greeting by letter, on a holy picture or postcard he writes: *May Jesus bless you and the Holy Virgin look after you. And please, do not cease to pray for* me. The image of Mary who protects us with her mantle has always accompanied Francis. Since he was a small boy he has prayed the *Sub tuum praesidium* learnt from his family and Salesian devotion. On the other hand, when the Bishop of Rome tells his brothers and sisters to *pray for me*, he is recognizing the prayerful subjectivity of the believing people who support his ministry.

Chapter 5
MARY AND THE PEOPLE OF THE WORLD

1. *The conversion or missionary reform of the Church from the periphery*

The Second Vatican Council presented the historical figure of the pilgrim and missionary people of God in the world (*LG* 9; 17) and led the reform of the Church through the word of the Holy Spirit (*LG* 4, *UR* 4). Throughout history, believers have been journeying in communion (*syn-hodos*) toward eschatological fullness. (*LG* 48, *GS* 45). The Council referred to ecclesial reform in its Decree on Ecumenism (*UR* 4). There it said that 'Christ summons the Church to continual reformation as she sojourns here on earth. The Church is always in need of this insofar as she is an institution of men here on earth' (*UR* 6).

In his Encyclical *Laudato Si'*, Francis said that he addressed *Evangelii Gaudium* 'to all the members of the Church *with the aim of encouraging ongoing missionary renewal*' (*LS* 3). His reform project has the gospel as its source and seeks to complete the reforms of Vatican II. With the reception of the Council and the Church's reform – not only the Roman Curia's – a new phase begins. The Pope is interested in continuity of reform. For Ghislain Lafont, 'the Francis event in itself is a development of the Second

Vatican Council event: a shift to a renewed understanding and practice of the Gospel.'¹

For the Pope, Vatican II did a re-reading of the Gospel and generated an irreversible dynamic:

> Vatican II was a re-reading of the Gospel in the light of contemporary culture. It produced a renewal movement that simply comes from the same Gospel. Its fruits are enormous... Yes, there are hermeneutics of continuity and discontinuity, but one thing is clear: the dynamic of reading the Gospel, actualising its message for today – which was typical of Vatican II – is absolutely irreversible.²

Francis calls us to '*missionary conversion*' (*EG* 30), a phrase which sums up the proposals of Aparecida on pastoral conversion and missionary renewal (*DA* 365–372). He calls for the reforming of ecclesial structures 'to make them more mission-orientated' (*EG* 27). This call implies the renewal of particular Churches and their pastoral plans (*EG* 30–31), and also conversion of the papacy and of the Church's central structures (*EG* 32). The reform is aimed at the Church being missionary. The *Ecclesial semper reformanda* is *Ecclesia in statu confessionis* and *in statu missionis*.

Francis reminds us: 'The Second Vatican Council presented ecclesial conversion as openness to a constant

---

1 G LAFONT, *Petit essai sur le temps du pape Francois*, Paris, Cerf, 2017, p. 26.

2 A SPADARO, '*Intervista a Papa Francisco*', op. cit. p. 467, [for English text cf. note 14, p. 26].

self-renewal born of fidelity to Jesus Christ' (*EG* 26; *UR* 6). The reformation of the Church seeks its spiritual and structural reward from its evangelical roots, so that it may be more faithful to Christ and the mission to evangelize. In an interview given in 2014 the Pope added: 'For me the big revolution is to go to the roots, recognize them and see what these roots have to say today.'[3] Ecclesial reform, marked by the Council, is a *ressourcement* for the return to the gospel source, and an *aggiornamento* for updating the current situation.[4] Francis wants to move forward on this journey of reform. Benedict XVI recognises this charism and says he is 'the man of practical reform.'[5]

In 2015, at the Fifth Congress of the Italian Church in Florence, Francis explained that 'the reform of the Church – and the Church is always *semper reformanda* – has nothing to do with pelagianism. It is not exhausted by the umpteenth plan to change structures. Instead it means grafting oneself onto, and rooting oneself in Christ, allowing oneself to be led by the Spirit. Then, all will be possible with inventiveness and creativity.'[6] He put the emphasis on the renewing work of the Spirit who renews and rejuvenates the Church (*LG* 4).

The task of *Ecclesia semper reformanda* is one that aims at taking a step forward on the journey of personal, communal

---

3 H. CYMERMAN, '*Entrevista al Papa Francisco*', *L'Osservatore romano* 20/6/2014, p. 6.

4 Cf. CH THEOBALD, *La réception du concile Vatican II. I. Accéder a la source*, Paris, Cerf, 2009, pp. 697–699.

5 BENEDICTO XVI, *Últimas conversaciones*, p. 238.

6 FRANCISCO, '*Sueño con una Iglesia inquieta*', *L'Osservatore romano*, 13/11/2015, p. 9.

and structural conversion toward holiness or the fullness of life in Christ. Some years ago, Bergoglio said: 'In the history of the Catholic Church the true reformers are those who change, transform, carry forward and revive the spiritual journey.'[7] The Blessed Virgin Mary and all the saints are outstanding figures who point the way to full communion with the Lord who is thrice holy.

Francis promotes a reformation of the Church and society from the outer fringes of poverty.

The Pope from the south of the South confirms what Dominican Yves Congar had already said in 1950: *many reforms come from the fringes.* Various reform movements were inspired by a return to evangelical poverty, and generated a commitment to the poor.[8]

> Initiatives often start at the periphery. They say that history develops at its margins, and that's right.. The margin is closer to the periphery than to the centre… But even if the majority of the reforms come from the periphery, and if reforms have no chance of succeeding unless they resonate with wide apostolic movements, they can only carry lead to reform *of the Church*, and reform *in the Church*, rather than a break, if they are taken up and incorporated by the church into its unity. This means, concretely, the agreement and approval of the central authorities, that

[7] JM Bergoglio; A Skorka, *Sobre el cielo y la tierra,* Buenos Aires, Sudamericana, 2013, p. 214.
[8] Cf. V Paglia, *Storia della povertá.*, Milan, Rizzoli, 2014, pp. 7–31, 222–238, 258–304, 351–419, 551–567.

> is, the consecration conferred on prophecy by apostolicity ... So in our obedience to the Spirit there is a kind of inherent tension, that is, an exchange or a relationship between two equally necessary poles. Ecclesial obedience attains its fullness only by including both poles and filling up the gap between them. The two poles are initiatives on the periphery and the benediction from the centre...[9]

When visiting the parish of Sts Zachary and Elizabeth on the outskirts of his new diocese, Francis said that reality is better understood from the periphery.[10] Bergoglio accompanied pastoral life in Buenos Aires' suburbs.[11] The Pope looks at the world situation from the poor people's point of view, and the poorest of the poor at that. The peripheries are not only privileged places of mission but are also hermeneutical horizons which help us to know the reality. Looking from the periphery, Francis calls us to seek an alternative social model of development, justice, and peace.[12]

---

9   Y CONGAR, *Verdadera y falsa reforma en la Iglesia*, op. cit., pp. 233, 234, 237, 240, also published in English as *True and False Reform in the Church*, trans. Paul Philibert, a Michael Glazier book published by Liturgical Press, Minesota, 2010..

10   Cf. JC SCANNONE, "*La realtà si capisce meglio guardandola non dal centro, ma dalle periferie*", in: *Francesco, Evangelii Gaudium*. Complete text and commentary by *La Civiltà Cattolica*, Milan, Ancora, 2014, pp. 183–196.

11   Cf. M DE VEDIA, *Francisco, El Papa del pueblo*, Buenos Aires, Planeta, 2013, pp. 129–149.

12   Cf. FRANCISCO, '*Discurso del Papa en el segundo encuentro mundial de los movimientos populares*', in: *Francisco en América*

2. Poor and for the poor. 'He looks on his servant in her lowliness... he raises the lowly'

The second chapter of *Evangelii Gaudium* analyzes some of the social challenges (*EG* 50–75), and its correlative chapter, the fourth, considers the social dimension of the kerygma regarding the kingdom of God (*EG* 180–181). The Pope says that many questions should be explored more deeply by everyone because he has no monopoly on the interpretation of reality (*EG* 16, 51, 184). With Paul VI's words in 1971 (*OA* 4), he asks Christian communities to discern the new challenges according to the gospel (*EG* 108). Francis questions the confidence placed in the dominant economic system while there are so many lives devoid of opportunities (*EG* 54). He denounces the new idolatry of money, a figure of the *mammon* of iniquity (Mt 6:24; Lk 16:13) and its profound anthropological crisis (*EG* 55). He says that 'money must serve, not rule!' (*EG* 58) and that unjust structures have a potential for 'disintegration and death' (*EG* 59).

In the fourth chapter, he picks up *another original contribution of the Latin American Church* developed from the document 'Poverty of the Church' at Medellín and found in Chapter 8 of Aparecida on 'The Kingdom of God and promoting human dignity' (*DA* 380–430). Our Church has considered and acted on the integration of human advancement, integral development and historical liberation in the gospel message and the evangelizing process. The

Latina¿ A qué nos convoca?, Buenos Aires, Patria Grande, 2016, pp. 89–105.

section of the document entitled 'Communal and societal repercussions of the kerygma' (*EG* 177–185) presents the social nature of the kingdom of God. It says that the missions includes 'the profound connection between evangelization and human advancement, which must necessarily find expression and develop in every work of evangelization' (*EG* 178). Here it assumes 'the option for those who are least, those whom society discards' (*EG* 195), in line with the option for the poor which is 'one of the distinguishing features of our Latin American and Caribbean Church' (*DA* 391). It is the deep bond which unites all the currents of our Latin American theology, symbolized in words like liberation, people, culture, the poor.

The Pope considers the themes of inclusion (*EG* 186–216) and peace (*EG* 218–258). In line with Aparecida (*DA* 391–398), *Evangelii Gaudium* presents faith in Christ who is poor, and the privileged place the poor have in God's heart: 'Our faith in Christ, who became poor, and was always close to the poor and the outcast, is the basis of our concern for the integral development of society's most neglected members' (*EG* 186). The section on the 'inclusion of the poor in society' *EG* 186–216) contains *the best statement of papal magisterium on Christ, the Church and the poor*. The principal claim, in line with Benedict XVI and Aparecida, says: 'God's heart has a special place for the poor, so much so that he himself 'became poor' (2 Cor 8:9) (*EG* 197).[13]

---

13   Cf. CM Galli, '*Los pobres en el corazón de Dios y del Pueblo de Dios. Del 'Pacto de las Catacumbas' a la Evangelii gaudium de Francisco*', in: X Pikaza – J Antunes, *El Pacto de las Catacumbas y*

With these theological and Christological foundations, the Bishop of Rome restates his dream:

> I want a Church which is poor and for the poor. They have much to teach us. Not only do they share in the *sensus fidei*, but in their difficulties they know the suffering Christ. We need to let ourselves be evangelized by them. The new evangelization is an invitation to acknowledge the saving power at work in their lives and to put them at the centre of the Church's pilgrim way. We are called to find Christ in them, to lend our voice to their causes, but also to be their friends, to listen to them, to speak for them, and to embrace the mysterious wisdom which God wishes to share with us through them (*EG* 198).

The option for the poor is a 'theological category' (*EG* 198) which 'must mainly translate into a privileged and preferential religious case' (*EG* 200). Many Christians are *poor in this world but rich in God in the faith* (cf. Jas 2:5).

In the Encyclical *Laudato Si'*, the Pope highlights the correlation between the cries of the poor and the groans of the earth (*LS* 2) and between care for the natural environment – environmental ecology, and care for human beings, especially the weakest – social ecology (*LS* 16). Both dimensions of a unique social-environmental crisis are calling for an integral ecology (*LS* 137). And he prays thus:

---

la misión de los pobres en la Iglesia, Estella, Verbo divino, 2015, pp. 259–296.

'O God of the poor, help us to rescue the abandoned and forgotten of this earth, so precious in your eyes' (*LS* 246).

The Magnificat is Mary's *exultet*, the handmaid's praise, the hymn to messianic joy, the song of the poor, the memory of mercy. *God's preferential love for the poor* is inscribed in Mary's song. The God of the Covenant casts the mighty from their thrones and raises the lowly, fills the starving with good things and sends the rich away empty. Mary is imbued with the spirit of the poor of Yahweh who place their hope in God alone. She proclaims the closeness of the evangelizing and liberating Messiah (Cf. Lk 4:16–21). The Church prays the song of Mary's praise and renews awareness of God's saving mercy for the poor. As a Mother she indicates 'what pedagogy should be used so that the poor 'feel at home' in every Christian Community. She creates communion and educates to a way of life shared in solidarity, in fraternity, in caring for and welcoming the other, especially if she is poor or in need' (*DA* 272). In our Latin American theology Mary is the Mother of the poor and a symbol of liberation.[14]

Francis looks at Mary as the poor woman and Mother of the defenceless. *Evangelii Gandium* says that she is the model of humility and that the Magnificat brings a homely warmth to our pursuit of justice.

> In her we see that humility and tenderness are not virtues of the weak but of the strong who need not treat others poorly in order to feel

---

14   Cf. MC Lucchetti Bingemer, *Maria madre di Dio e madre dei poveri*, Assisi, Citadella, 1989.

> important themselves. Contemplating Mary, we realise that she who praised God for 'bringing down the mighty form their thrones' and 'sending the rich away empty' (Lk 1:52–53) is also the one who brings a homely warmth to our pursuit of justice (*EG* 288).

The Aparecida Document indicates helpless *migrants* in the option for the poor and the excluded (*DA* 411–416). The Church accompanies them and welcomes them with its ministry to human mobility. In the ongoing 'encyclical' of his gestures, Francis embodies the *Marian, Samaritan, merciful and empathetic Church*. His constant solicitude for migrants, refugees, the displaced responds to a new sign of this time and the process of multi-dimensional globalization. One out of seven people in the world is displaced from his or her original home. When visiting Lampedusa, Juarez and Lesbos, the Pope has condemned the globalization of indifference, human trafficking, the avoidable deaths of so many individuals. When establishing the *Dicastery for integral human development* he reserved the secretarial office to himself. It is dedicated to those suffering forced migration. Like Jesus, the successor of Peter expresses God's love for victims. His decisions and gestures, with their real and symbolic effectiveness, do not solve these structural dramas but they indicate the direction for change. We Christians recognize the face and voice of Jesus in migrants: I *was a stranger and you welcomed me* (Mt 25:35).

3. La Morenita: *Our Lady of Guadalupe and the peoples of America*

At Aparecida, Bergoglio collaborated in recognising that the appearance of Our Lady at Guadalupe was the decisive event for first evangelisation. The Conference re-interpreted it in the light of Pentecost. God's breath acted in Mary to beget a new people in Christ.

> Mary is the great missionary, continuer of her Son's mission, who forms missionaries. As she gave birth to the Saviour of the world she brought the Gospel to our Americas. In the Guadalupe event, together with the humble Juan Diego, she presided over Pentecost, which opened us to the gifts of the Spirit (*DA* 269).

The Christ of God becomes present in Latin America through Mary, the most beautiful sign of his loving closeness and the woman most sought out by the heart of the people that is *God's shrine. At Guadalupe, God gave Latin American to the Virgin and the Virgin to Latin America.* This is noted in the daily life and common culture of many individuals, families and peoples. The Latin American Church has an original modern Marian piety with Iberian roots with a *mestizo*, mixed cultural face that was not conceived by ancient or medieval Christianity as it was in European Churches.

The Pope expresses its roots in love of the Mother of God and Latin American Marian piety by quoting the *Nican Mopohua* account and inviting us to contemplate the figure of Our Lady of Guadalupe. Through her image and shrine she extends her loving gaze to all members of the people of God. The Pope says: 'As she did with Juan Diego, Mary offers them maternal comfort and love, and whispers in their ear: 'Let your heart not be troubled. Am I not here, who am your Mother?" (*EG* 286).

His message forms part of the Latin American tradition that at Puebla contemplated Guadalupe as the symbol of our historical and cultural originality. In the homily at the Mass of the Virgin of Guadalupe, celebrated in 2013 in St Peter's Basilica, the Pope indicated this *mestizo* inculturation:

> She wanted to appear as a mestizo woman. She wanted to show that she was of mixed race like our people: she wanted to show she was pregnant, just as she showed herself to her cousin St Elizabeth. She wanted to show her devotion with these hands joined but open at the same time like a paten, receiving all the people. She wanted to show herself not as a learned person, bishop, priest or nun but as an Indian going off to work to feed his wife and children. And with simplicity she wanted to tell all of us, by her mestizo face and her womb about to give birth, with these joined yet open hands in prayer, that she is with our American peoples. Today we give you thanks; thank you Mother for this encounter, thank you for having appeared to this America which is born of mixed race, thanks for bringing us Jesus in the same way you brought him in your womb to your cousin.

In Chapter 4 of *Evangelii Gaudium*, Francis develops the theme of dialogue for peace and presents four principles that guide a *culture of encounter* in order to overcome social tensions (*EG* 217–237).[15] His theology of society and history focuses on a call to build up peoples through 'a peaceful and multifaceted culture of encounter' (*EG* 220). The Bishop of Rome unfurls a political anthropology inspired by Christian humanism, which he expounded systematically in 2010 in his address *We as citizens, we as people* on the *Day of Social Ministry in Buenos Aires* at the beginning of the nation's Bicentenary.[16] He maintains that we need to shift from being passive inhabitants to being responsible citizens who have rights and duties, and cultivate belonging to a people who share a common historical destiny.[17]

Francis briefly develops four principles that help develop a *culture of encounter*: time is greater than space, unity prevails over conflict, realities are more important than ideas, the whole is greater than the part. These help forge common projects and contribute to peace. The fourth principle, the whole is greater than the part (*EG* 234–237), analyzes the tensions between globalization and localization. The way to a synthesis which overcomes tensions is not reflected in the 'global' which 'need not stifle, nor the particular' which

---

15 Cf. JC Scannone, '*Cuatro principios para la construcción de un pueblo según el Papa Francisco*', Stromata 71/1 (2015) pp. 13–27.
16 Cf. JM Bergoglio, *Nosotros como ciudadanos, nosotros como pueblo*, Buenos Aires, Claretiana, 2013.
17 Cf. D Fares, '*La antropologia politica di Papa Francesco*', La Civiltá Cattolica 3928 (2014) pp. 345–360; *Papa Francesco é come un bambú. Alle radice della cultura dell'incontro*, Rome, Ancora, 2014.

does not 'prove barren' (*EG* 235). For Francis, the *polyhedron* represents the culture of encounter. The polyhedron reflects the convergence of all its parts, each of which preserves its distinctiveness (*EG* 236). By uniting these distinct parts in the universal and at the same time preserving what is peculiar to them, this culture builds bridges to overcome the abysses.

The appearance of an image of the Virgin of Guadalupe on Juan Diego's cloak is a prophetic sign of Mary's embrace of all the inhabitants of the vast American lands, those already in existence and those yet to come. This embrace indicated the journey that has characterized America as a land where different peoples can co-exist and which is capable of welcoming migrants, as also the peoples and the poor and marginalized of all eras. America is a generous land. Today myriads arrive at their new destinations with their beliefs and values, re-creating their identities in new places. Many are helping to give new energy to the Catholic Faith and popular piety of other continents, becoming spontaneous missionaries in Europe or Asia. They bring with them not only their poverties, needs and sins but also their riches, values and virtues, especially the gift of the Catholic Faith manifested in its popular piety. They can help re-create the faith where it has grown weak and 'offer a valuable missionary contribution' (*DA* 415). Wherever Mexicans come together, a spontaneous devotion to the Virgin of Guadalupe is born. A missionary Church which goes forth must integrate migrants with their cultural identity and their popular piety in the new evangelization of the cities of the whole world.

In Philadelphia, Francis evoked North American history from the arrival of the colonists, to provide a foundation for respect owed the cultural identity and religious freedom of all citizens, old and new.[18] Within this framework the Pope situated pastoral mercy for migrants, refugees ad displaced persons. At his meeting with North American bishops the Pope renewed his thanks and asked them for fraternal welcome.[19]

Migrations are a new challenge for recognizing otherness, building bridges and embracing differences. Faith leads us to look at and lover the *other* (*alter*) as a *brother* (*frater*). Through Jesus we call on God as 'Our Father' (Mt 6:9) and embrace others, since 'we are all brothers' (Mt 23:9). On 5 November 2016, Francis spoke to participants at the Third World Meeting of Popular Movements. He invited them to show the love which builds bridges, opens, includes, integrates.

> Let all the walls come down. All of them. We should not let ourselves be fooled. Let us continue to build bridges between peoples, bridges which allow us to pull down the walls of exclusion and exploitation. Let us confront Terror with Love. The '3 Ts,' that cry of yours that I make my own, has something of this humble, but at the same time strong and healing understanding. A bridge project of the peoples

---

18   Cf. FRANCIS, *From Cuba to Philadelphia. A mission of love*, Vatican, Librería Editrice Vaticana, 2015, pp. 385–391.

19   Cf. FRANCIS, *From Cuba to Philadelphia*, p. 317.

in contrast to the wall project of money; a project that points to integral development.[20]

We are members of the pilgrim and migrant Church throughout the world. We are called to carry out a mediating service which helps build bridges of encounter and peace. The Church co-operates in facilitating integration and avoiding exclusion. In America only the *Virgen Morita*, the Brown Virgin Mother of all the American peoples, can intercede to move hearts for building bridges between North and South. In 1992 the Fifth Centenary of the Faith in America helped take up a new evangelization. The Church spent nine years preparing for it. In 1531, four decades after 1492, came the Guadalupe event through which Mary, the great missionary, 'brought the Gospel to America' (*DA* 269). Now, shall we turn our gaze to 2031?[21]

4. Salve Regina, mater misericordiae: *the style of Marian tenderness*

The mercy of our God comes to us through the motherly tenderness of Mary and the Church. Our peoples 'find God's affection and love in the face of Mary' (*DA* 265). In Mary 'the merciful dimension of the Church's motherhood' shines forth.[22] From ancient times she has been called

---

20 FRANCISCO, '*Sembradores del cambio. Discurso en el III Encuentro mundial de los movimientos populares*', *L'Osservatore romano*, 11/11/2016, pp. 6–9, 7.

21 Cf. CM GALLI, '*Orientar nuestra mirada hacia el futuro (de 2031)*', *L'Osservatore romano*, 17/6/2017, pp. 2–3.

22 FRANCISCO, *Carta a la XXXVI Asamblea General del Consejo Episcopal Latinoamericano*, p. 3.

the *Mother of Divine Mercy*, *Our Lady of Mercy*, *Mother of Mercy*. She welcomes, shelters and cares for all her children in all their needs, wounds and distress. Current Mariology is reflecting on Mary as *Mother of Mercy*.[23] We perceive, in Mary's heart, 'the tender mercy of our God' (Lk 1:28). Mary knows the mercy of God in the depths of her being. Her sharing in the passion and death of her Son, become a sign of contradiction, is like a sword piercing her heart (cf. Lk 2:35). The Sorrowful Mother shares in a special way in the sacrifice which reveals the paternal and maternal heart of God. The Mother of the Crucified Lord experienced the kiss of mercy as she rightfully should. She testifies to the fact that mercy reaches everyone and excludes no one. Her feminine and motherly sensitivity has a special ability to reach out to those who accept merciful love from a mother. The motherly tenderness of the *Theotókos* infuses a special note of gentleness. Nothing is more gentle than mercy, as Francis reminded us on 8 December in the Piazza di Spagna in Rome. The prayer *Salve Regina* also asks Mary not to tire of turning her merciful eyes toward us, showing us Jesus, blessed fruit of her womb 'radiant face of God's mercy' (*MM* 22). In the Bull *Misericordia Vultus*, the Pope says that the sweetness of her countenance helps us to:

> Rediscover the joy of God's tenderness. No one has penetrated the profound mystery of

---

23 Cf. J GARCÍA PAREDES, '*Mater Misericordiae. María, ícono de la misericordia de Dios*', Ephemerides Mariologicae 65 (2015) pp. 277–293; S PETRELLA, '*Mater Misericordiae: Maria beneficiaria e testimone della Misericordia. Alcune riflessioni teologiche*', Marianum 189/190 (2016) pp. 171–230.

> the Incarnation like Mary. Her entire life was patterned after the presence of mercy made flesh. The Mother of the Crucified and Risen One has entered the sanctuary of divine mercy because she participated intimately in the mystery of His love (*MV* 24).

Among the peoples of the world, 'by her maternal charity (Mary) cares for the brethren of her Son, who still journey on earth surrounded by dangers and distress, until they are led into the happiness of their true home' (*LG* 62). Latin American pastoral life has a pastoral style focused on maternal tenderness: 'Our peoples... find God's affection and love in the face of Mary' (*DA* 265). Since 1531, on the Tepeyac hill, the *brown face of the Virgin of Guadalupe*, holds her people in the pupil of her eyes and wraps them in the fold of her mantle. Since 1717, near the Paraiba River, the *black face of Our Lady of Aparecida* invites us to cast our nets to rescue those drowning in oblivion and bring them to the source of abundant life. Pilgrimages are spiritual and emotional gestures which express the life of faith and Communion of the Saints. The pilgrim sets out for the shrine moved by faith, walks enlivened by hope and on arrival enjoys the encounter and contemplates lovingly: 'the pilgrim's gaze rests on an image that symbolizes God's affection and closeness. Love pauses, contemplates mystery, and enjoys it in silence...' (*DA* 260).

Popular Latin American culture is marked by the heart, affection, and bonds. A Marian evangelizing pedagogy is a warm, binding, familiar kind of pastoral ministry.[24] The people of God needs a woman who is a mother, not only a model. The Blessed Virgin is the type and mother of the faithful people. With this Mariology, Puebla stated that Mary 'is the point of connection between heaven and earth. Without Mary the gospel is disincarnated, disfigured and turns into an ideology, into spiritualist rationalism' (*DP* 301). The Pope shares this theological and pastoral view. He reminds us in his pastoral Exhortation that we learn from the Mother of God that 'there is a Marian 'style' to the Church's work of evangelization… the revolutionary nature of love and tenderness' (*EG* 288).

This is the context for a devotion which Jorge Bergoglio made known in Buenos Aires and which has spread throughout Argentina. It is an image of *Mary Undoer of Knots* (*Knoten löserin*), depicted in a painting of Bavarian origin in baroque style. Bergoglio came to know of it when he received a copy on a Christmas card. He recalls: 'I liked the image, asked for more and they sent them to me. I then had it printed in Buenos Aires and suggested that the University of Salvador send it out as a Christmas greeting.' In 1992 he included it in the booklet for his episcopal ordination. Francis recalls that a decisive step for its diffusion was the painting of a replica of the original picture and its enthronement in *San José de Talan* church in the archdiocese. Since then it has become a small shrine.

---

24 Cf. J ALLIENDE, '*María educadora de discípulos misioneros en la pastoral de América Latina y el Caribe*', in: CELAM, *María, Madre de discípulos*, pp. 113–240.

Elsewhere he showed that this devotion to *Mary Undoer of Knots* joins other new expressions of popular urban piety which open the way to God, providing a way to heal wounds and personal distress of a spiritual, emotional and psychological nature.[25] On the back of his printed version we read: 'By her obedience Mary undoes the knots we all carry through our disobedience.'

'*This is the first Marian celebration... the Undoer of Knots...*' the Pope told his Marian colleague.[26] As the Council reminds us, St Justin and St Irenaeus offer an antithetical parallel between Eve and Mary, tied to the Pauline theology of the two Adams (*LG* 56). This comparison is made in relation to sin and righteousness in the Letter to the Romans, and on the basis of the death-resurrection opposition in the First Letter to the Corinthians (Rom 5:12–21; 1 Cor 15:12–58). St Paul teaches: 'For just as by one man's disobedience the many were made sinners, so by the one man's obedience the many will be made righteous' (Rom 5:19). And also: 'for as all die in Adam, so all will be made alive in Christ (1 Cor 15:22).

The Virgin Queen and Mother of Mercy is our 'life, our sweetness and our hope.' She reflects the light of hope which comes from the 'sun from on high' through 'the loving mercy of our God.' Francis contemplates the Church as *mysterium lunae*. On 11 September 1962, John XXIII recalled the symbolism of the Easter candle and directed his gaze to Christ the Light of the World. He focused the Council's

25 Cf. GALLI, *Dio vive in città, pp.* 203–212.
26 AWI MELLO, *Ella es mi mamá*, p. 160.

subject matter on the words '*Lumen Christi, Lumen Ecclesiae, Lumen gentium.*' At the opening of the Council he said: 'This is only the dawn and already the first rays of the sun in the east begin to warm our hearts.'[27] The dawn of the Second Vatican Council's reform according to the gospel of Christ is lit up through the brilliance of the dawning of Mary and the Church. If John XXIII glimpsed the conciliar dawning, Francis accompanies the Church in this new stage (*EG* 1) to better reflect the Sun of Christ in the brightness of the midday sun.

One dawn calls to the other dawn. Catholic piety calls the Virgin the *Morning Star*. Mary is light and hence the Liturgy calls her 'the Dawn.' As light she proclaims that the great Light who is Christ will come. The metaphor of light belongs to the symbol of *Our Lady of Fatima*. In his visit to the Portuguese Shrine for the centenary of the event, Francis prayed for the light and warmth of God's mercy to give rise to peace in the world in accordance with the message of Fatima.[28]

Hail Holy Queen,

Blessed Virgin of Fatima,

Our Lady of the Immaculate Heart ...

Hail Mother of Mercy,

Lady robed in white ...

Blessed are you among women,

27 Cf. A MELLONI, *Papa Giovanni. Un cristiano e il suo concilio*, Turin, Einaudi, 2009, p. 333.
28 Cf. E BUENO DE LA FUENTE, *El mensaje de Fátima. La misericordia de Dios: el triunfo del amor en los dramas de la historia*, Burgos, Monte Carmelo, 2013.

> You are the image of the Church dressed in Easter light…
> Prophecy of the merciful Love of the Father,
> Teacher of the Message of
> Good News of the Son,
> Sign of the burning Fire of the Spirit…
> Show us the strength of your protective mantle[29]

Mary is the Dawn of the gospel and, at this stage of history, the Star of the first and of the new evangelization. Just as Paul VI called Mary 'Star of evangelization' (*EN* 82) our regional Church has called her 'Star of the First and New evangelization' (*SD* 15). Mary, our life, our sweetness and our hope, is the Dawn of the luminous morning of the gospel in the world, and the Star in the historical nights of evangelisation until the Lord comes.

---

29 Francisco, '*Oración a la Virgen de Fátima*', *L'Osservatore romano* (Argentinian edition), 20/5/2017, p. 16.

www.ingramcontent.com/pod-product-compliance
Lightning Source LLC
Chambersburg PA
CBHW051950290426
44110CB00015B/2190